WARRINGTON
FOR
EVER!

WARRINGTON FOR EVER!

A Portrait of the Town and its People

by

Alan Crosby and Janice Hayes

Wharncliffe Books

Published in association with
Warrington Library, Museum and Archives Service

First published in Great Britain in 2006 by
Wharncliffe Local History
an imprint of
Pen & Sword Books Ltd
47 Church Street
Barnsley
South Yorkshire
S70 2AS

ISBN 1 90342 561 1

Typeset in Bodoni by
Phoenix Typesetting, Auldgirth, Dumfriesshire

Printed and bound in England by
Biddles Ltd, Kings Lynn

Pen & Sword Books Ltd incorporates the Imprints of Pen & Sword Aviation, Pen
& Sword Maritime, Pen & Sword Military, Wharncliffe Local History, Pen &
Sword Select, Pen & Sword Military Classics and Leo Cooper.

For a complete list of Pen & Sword titles please contact
PEN & SWORD BOOKS LIMITED
47 Church Street, Barnsley, South Yorkshire, S70 2AS, England
E-mail: enquiries@pen-and-sword.co.uk
Website: www.pen-and-sword.co.uk

CONTENTS

ACKNOWLEDGEMENTS

The authors would like to acknowledge all those who have made this volume possible.

This volume has been compiled from official records and archives in the care of Warrington Borough Council's Library, Museum & Archives Service and from photographs taken by professional and amateur photographers and from the family albums and reminiscences of Warringtonians.

The majority of illustrations in this volume are taken from the extensive collections held at Warrington Central Library and Museum. We would like to thank all staff past and present for their help and for ensuring that these important collections are preserved.

Acknowledgements are also due to various community organizations, including the Loushers Lane Memories Group, the Latchford History Group, the Howley Heritage Group and the Burtonwood Association. The Heritage Lottery Fund generously supported the recent 'Gateway through Time' Project, whose co-ordinator Heather McAlpine has helped to gather many more local memories to add to the official sources.

This volume would not have been possible without the contribution of local photographers. Every effort has been made to trace the copyright holders but the Museum & Archives Service would be interested to learn of further details or sources of the images featured.

Welcome to Warrington town centre 19091! Crowds in Buttermarket Street wait to greet King Edward VII.

CHAPTER ONE

THE DEVELOPMENT OF WARRINGTON: A HISTORICAL OVERVIEW

What makes Warrington and 'Warringtonians' special? How did the town emerge as one of the leading industrial and commercial centres of the region? Who are the people, famous, infamous or 'ordinary' who have helped to shape its history?

Today the borough of Warrington incorporates twenty-two distinct wards stretching from Culcheth in the north to Lymm in the south and from Penketh in the west to Birchwood in the east. Between these are the old established areas of Howley and Latchford and newer suburbs on the fringes

The bridge over the River Mersey at Warrington had given the town its regional importance by the time of this 1580s drawing. Built at the expense of the earl of Derby in 1495, the three-arched bridge brought travellers past the cluster of half-timbered houses and shops in Bridge Street, past the Jesus church of the Austin Friars (left) or to the village off Church Street with its parish church (right).

of the town centre itself. Early twenty-first-century Warrington is a self-governing authority within the county of Cheshire but for much of its history the borough was part of Lancashire. The local government reorganization of 1974 created an enlarged borough straddling the River Mersey, incorporating many former historic communities on its borders, all with their own unique history and character. This new 'unity in diversity' has enriched the identity of the modern town.

Among Warrington's citizens (or 'Warringtonians') are individuals who dedicated themselves to serving Warrington and its communities, devoting their energies to making this a better place. Others were notorious characters – criminals and ne'er-do-wells – who cannot be said to have had the public good in mind, but nonetheless have their place in history. Still others were celebrities and larger-than-life figures who, from a Warrington base or birthplace, made fortunes or set their stamp upon their times.

This book is a celebration of Warrington in all its many aspects, giving a flavour or a taste of the wealth of history which lies in its streets and buildings and open spaces, and introducing some of the key themes which helped to shape and mould its past and its present.

Location, location, location is the key to Warrington's origin and its importance. The town grew at the point where the River Mersey meets the sea – in the past, the upper limit of navigation for vessels – and also at what was, until the mid-nineteenth century, the lowest point at which the river could be bridged. Here, the ancient north–south highway, one of the great trunk routes of England from the prehistoric period to the present day, crosses the river and intersects with an important east–west route, bringing people and goods along the Mersey valley by land or, later, by water. The bridges at Warrington have been one of the nodal points on the national transport network from the Roman period onwards. Even today, although

The importance of Warrington to the national transport network was emphasized in the Civil Wars of the mid-seventeenth century. Leading Royalists and Parliamentarians lodged in the town, including Oliver Cromwell who stayed in the central cottage in Church Street in 1648 in one of the last strategic campaigns of the wars.

Thelwall viaduct has provided a comparable strategic point a little way upstream, the meeting of routes in central Warrington (and the consequent heavy traffic flows) demonstrates the continuing importance of this spot, while the ceaseless rushing of trains through Bank Quay station and over the great high-level bridge just to the south reinforces that same message.

During the Roman period, though there was settlement on the north bank of the river, the main focus of activity was on the south side, at Wilderspool, where there was a large industrial and commercial centre, with potteries, iron-working, lead-working and other trades. This was a military and civilian supply depot, which sent goods as far afield as Hadrian's Wall, and there was also a sizeable town close by, on the slopes towards Stockton Heath. A very important Roman road led northwards from Middlewich, through Wilderspool and over the river, almost certainly by a bridge, before striking out across south Lancashire to Wigan and on to the northern borders of the empire. Other roads linked Wilderspool with Chester and Manchester, and probably with Derbyshire. For three centuries Roman material has been found in abundance in the Wilderspool area, either in the course of building work and civil engineering projects or during organized archaeological excavations, and more finds continue to be made. Among the special treasures is a celebrated actor's face-mask, made of pottery, which is unique in Britain and is now in Warrington Museum.

We know comparatively little about the area in the period after the Romans left, but by the time of the Norman Conquest there was clearly a

The River Mersey had become a major traffic artery by the late eighteenth century as it was linked to the new canal network. Warrington also had a thriving fishing industry with catches of 'sturgeon, green backs, mullets, seals, sand eels, lobsters, prawns and the best and largest cockles in all England'. This 1792 view shows (left) the old St James's Church, (centre) Howley water mill and (right) the parish church.

well-established pattern of agricultural communities on both sides of the river, with Warrington itself serving as a central place and local administrative and political focus. The remarkable dedication of the parish church reveals its great antiquity – St Elphin is an obscure Anglo-Saxon saint, but his very shadowiness suggests that we can trace the origins of the church, and the holiness of its site, back to the earliest days of Christianity in the area, in the seventh century. Winwick church is similarly ancient, and is associated with a series of legends and features such as holy wells, normally taken to indicate a very early religious site. It is considered, with reasonable confidence, that somewhere in the vicinity of Winwick was the great battle of Maserfelth, in AD 642, when the Northumbrians were defeated by an alliance of the Mercians and the Welsh. From at least AD 900 at Warrington itself there was a defended and fortified complex on Mote Hill, immediately beside the parish church. From there the hundred of Warrington, an administrative district extending across south–central Lancashire, was administered, and the vital river crossing and meeting of routeways was guarded. The strategic and political importance of the site was further emphasized by the construction, in the early years of the tenth century, of a new fortress beside the river at Thelwall, as part of a chain of military sites extending from Chester to Manchester and into the Peak District along the

Rush hour traffic on Warrington Bridge in 1910 may seem relatively light to modern eyes but there were already signs that the structure would soon become a bottleneck. Warrington's councillors were far-sighted enough to replace it with the present 30 foot wide structure completed in 1913, but they could never have envisaged the national growth of road traffic within a century.

Warrington's road, waterway and rail links had established the town as a major industrial centre by the late nineteenth century. One of the main industrial zones was concentrated around Bank Quay, with its river and main north–south rail connections.

frontier between English and Scandinavian territories. Indeed, the very name 'Mersey' means 'boundary river'.

Political and administrative significance went hand in hand with commercial importance, reinforced and enhanced by the key route centre which Warrington had become. It is likely that there was already a market here before the Norman Conquest, for the widening of the road outside the gates of the parish church represents Warrington's earliest market place. It is an intriguing turn of historical fate that one edge of this ancient trading place is now occupied by Sainsbury's car park. Today the parish church and the old market place may appear to be in something of a backwater, away from the centre of the modern town, but during the Anglo-Saxon period, when there was no bridge over the river, and until the thirteenth century the main route from the south crossed the Mersey at a ford at Latchford and then followed what is now Howley Lane. This original market place was thus adjacent to the junction of this road with the east–west route now marked by Church Street and Manchester Road. In the early thirteenth century the more direct route, via Wilderspool Causeway and Bridge Street, began to return to favour and by 1285 a bridge had been constructed. This channelled traffic away from the old market place, and instead the crossroads which is now Market Gate became the town's focus. In the later thirteenth century, therefore, a new market place was constructed close to the crossroads, and that in Church Street lost its trading activities – though it remained the focus of the famous Warrington fairs for centuries to come.

The town grew, slowly but steadily, expanding westwards around the new market place and becoming one of only three urban centres in Lancashire to acquire a religious house. The Augustinian friary was founded sometime

Despite its new industrial status Warrington was still a thriving market town in the 1840s. Here country traders peddle their wares in front of the distinctive sixteenth-century Barley Mow Inn. By the 1850s Warrington had grown dissatisfied with its medieval-style open market. Civic pride, a desire for progress and better hygiene led the Corporation to purchase the market tolls from the lord of the manor and redevelop the area.

By the late nineteenth century more heavy industries were concentrated at Bewsey, Whitecross and especially off Dallam Lane near the Cheshire Lines rail route between Liverpool and Manchester.

before 1292 by William le Boteler, its location, immediately behind Bridge Street, explained by the need of the friars to solicit alms and charitable gifts from passers-by. The busy thoroughfare leading from the bridge to the market place was ideal for such a purpose. In this period, too, Warrington was granted its first borough charter, though its date is unknown – it may have been as early as the 1220s – but we do know that in the 1290s there was a bitter dispute between the citizens and the Boteler lords of the manor, because the people of the town wanted to exercise a greater degree of self-government than the lord was prepared to allow. In 1300 the citizens had to concede, so although the town was technically still a free borough, in reality it remained strictly under the control of its manorial lords, a position which prevailed for no less than 547 years more, until the early years of Victoria's reign.

Despite this setback, the growth of the town continued, and by 1500 Warrington had established its position as one of the leading centres of north-west England. The documentary records, from which we reconstruct the history of the area, improve in quality and quantity from the sixteenth century onwards. We have plenty of evidence of inns and innkeepers, shops and shopkeepers, to point to the business and commercial life of the town.

By the late twentieth century Warrington had seen its heavy industries follow the national pattern of decline and eventual closure. New uses were needed for these derelict sites and this former tannery and brewery off Winwick Road and Dallam Lane were to become the new stadium for Warrington Wolves and Tesco's supermarket.

Contemporary accounts tell of the major damage and destruction in the Church Street area during the Civil War sieges in 1642 and 1643. Records reveal the comfortable lifestyles of leading citizens, with their rich furnishings and fine jewels and plate, and there are darker stories from court papers; episodes of violent crime and petty thieving; of subversive gossip in alehouses and brawling in the streets.

Yet nobody could have predicted the scale or impact of the changes which Warrington and the surrounding areas would experience from the end of the seventeenth century onwards. A combination of circumstances – location, transport connections, proximity to raw materials and the entrepreneurial talents of individuals – allowed the town to emerge as one of the first major industrial centres in Britain, a process well under way long before the Industrial Revolution. The nearness of the Cheshire saltfields and the Lancashire coalfields provided the impetus to industrial growth, giving ready supplies of raw materials and fuel, while the improvement of the estuary in the 1690s, and the creation of the Mersey and Irwell Navigation in the early eighteenth century, dramatically enhanced Warrington's role as a transport centre. Raw materials could be brought in from further afield, whether copper and lead ores from North Wales or exotic imports of palm oil and olive oil destined for the infant soap and chemical industries. As transport technology became more sophisticated, Warrington was a focus for

Not Constable's haywain but a rustic scene recorded by local artist Oswald Garside in 1926. Intended as inspiration for his paintings, Garside's photographs reveal that away from the immediate town centre Warrington's villages were still isolated communities, unchanged by the passage of time.

The first integration of Warrington and its outlying districts began with the public transport network. Trams served limited routes between 1901 and 1935 but these were replaced by motor buses to serve the new council housing estates. By the late twentieth century a network of motorways, express ways, local distributor roads and the old highways linked the town centre with established villages and New Town Development areas.

canal, turnpike road and, later, early railway schemes. Along the riverside, from Sankey through Bank Quay to Arpley and Howley, a new industrial zone emerged, beginning as early as the 1690s. Potteries, soapworks, metal-working, tanning, glass, chemicals and boatbuilding, among many other trades, were all to be found by 1800. In the second half of the eighteenth century some of the old domestic trades, such as wire-drawing, file-cutting, pin-making and fustian-cutting, began to expand. Production started to shift from backyard sheds and backrooms of houses into factories or larger workshops. Warrington acquired a broad economic base, unique in the region, for virtually every significant industry was represented. It was less specialized in its economic structure than any other town in the region, and that gave it a commercial resilience and a cushion against the ups and downs of the economic cycle which were so greatly to damage the well-being of towns dependent on a single industry.

The effect of this remarkable economic transformation was immediately felt in the townscape and the landscape. The town grew rapidly in population, from perhaps 3,000 at the start of the eighteenth century to 11,000 a century later, and 25,000 in 1850. But these figures relate only to the old town. Some parts of Greater Warrington, the area covered by the present

This view of London Road, Stockton Heath, from Victoria Square in 1897 is almost unrecognizable today. Apart from the lack of traffic the character of the high street has changed beyond recognition. All over the town shopkeepers ceased to live on the premises and London Road itself became dominated by retail operations.

borough, were growing even faster, so that formerly small and purely rural communities such as Culcheth and Burtonwood, Stockton Heath or Grappenhall, Lymm or Sankey, began to expand, acquiring industrial employment in mining or metal-working or emerging as favoured new residential areas for commuters and people who once chose to live in the congested heart of the town but now wanted peace and quiet and open space. Early nineteenth-century Warrington was an increasingly dirty, polluted, noisy and crowded place. By the 1850s the major problems posed by the filthy Mersey, the smoke-choked atmosphere, the squalid housing, the deplorable public health record, the insanitary sewerless courts and yards and the chaotic traffic of busy streets were uncongenial to better-off residents. Some fled to Palmyra Square and the nearby oases, but many favoured a move to 'the Cheshire side', and from this time onwards the rural townships south of the river had a special status as a desirable place to live. The town itself was criss-crossed with new railway lines, and alongside those came new industrial premises – the great wireworks of the mid-Victorian period, the breweries and the chemical plants. But still all the traffic within the town and just passing through was concentrated on the all-too-narrow bridge and the no less congested Bridge Street.

Town government became a pressing issue. In 1813 the Warrington Police Commissioners, a body made up of the town's leading ratepayers, were established by Act of Parliament to tackle the great backlog of social and environmental problems. They and their officials worked hard, taking steps to provide a police force, a sewerage system, street-paving and street-lighting, refuse collection, a fire brigade and proper regulation of the market. In 1847 they were superseded by the new Borough Council established upon the granting of a new charter by Queen Victoria. Over the next sixty years many other features of civilized urban living were introduced, including gas, water and electricity supplies, the first serious efforts to regulate housing quality, public health reforms with the new hospital, and the pioneering free public library and museum, the first in the country to be paid for from the rates. In 1900 Warrington, then with a population of over 65,000, became a self-governing county borough.

Inevitably, the twentieth century brought change no less dramatic or remarkable than any which had gone before. Each of the town's great industries – wire-working, soap-making, metal-working of all sorts, brewing, cotton-weaving and tanning – could be said to have reached a peak of importance in the middle years of the century, before undergoing decline,

This view of 1963 shows the town centre before its planned redevelopment. In the 1930s Marks & Spencer's store had been constructed with a false frontage in anticipation of the widening of Sankey Street to cope with the increasing volume of traffic. The redevelopment of Golden Square in the 1970s and 1980s produced a traffic-free shopping environment, serviced by an inner ring road, adjacent bus station and multi-storey car park.

At the turn of the twenty-first century the pace of change has accelerated as Golden Square benefits from a second multi-million pound redevelopment. These properties off Horsemarket Street had disappeared in the 1970s to make way for the inner ring road between Golbourne Street and Scotland Road. By mid-2006 this scene became the site of Warrington's impressive new bus interchange.

disappearance or at least transformation between 1950 and 2000. That wire-working has gone, brewing is confined to Burtonwood, soap-making is almost entirely automated and the biggest cotton mill is now a shopping centre illustrates the decline and dwindling of the old industrial base. But that one of the most extensive and busiest retailing zones in Britain is on the northern edge of the town, and that Warrington has one of the highest growth rates and lowest unemployment rates in the north, and that business parks and office developments are thickly scattered across the borough, reflects the fact that the fundamental advantages of location and economic diversity remain as significant today as they have always been. Though its traditional industries gradually disappeared, Warrington did not rely on any one of them to the extent that its basic economic well-being was eroded. Its unity in diversity continues to be a powerful theme.

In the mid-1960s Warrington was designated as a new town, to receive overspill population from Merseyside and Manchester and to develop a gleaming new infrastructure of transport and community facilities and amenities based on the framework provided by the motorway network, then approaching completion. The box of the M6, M56 and M62, and their link roads, gave the town an unrivalled position at one of the most important nodes of the national network. The designated new town embraced not only the old borough but also an extensive area of suburban parishes and semi-rural communities north of the river, and a broad swathe of Cheshire countryside to the south. In 1974 the area was given its administrative unity by the creation of the enlarged borough, a district within Cheshire, and in 1998 the borough was given unitary status and so is once again self-governing.

Today Warrington borough has a population of just under 200,000, of whom only about a quarter live in the area of the old borough. With its buoyant economy, great retail and business parks, large new residential areas and much-improved infrastructure it has many of the elements we would associate with any successful twentieth- and twenty-first-century new town, but it also has a long and rich history, an important legacy of buildings of historic or architectural interest, valuable and cherished natural landscapes, and a highly diverse character. These, and the people who have made it and continue to make it, ensure that Warrington is conscious of its past as well as its present and its future.

CHAPTER TWO

TELLING THE STORY: THE OFFICIAL AND THE UNOFFICIAL SOURCES

How can we find out about Warrington's unique history and the lives of Warringtonians? Although it is always important, and interesting, to look at the published work of historians over the decades, from the anti-quarians who wrote about aspects of Warrington history two centuries ago to present-day writers with their different perspectives and approaches, it is particularly rewarding, and fascinating, to use the original sources – the contemporary documents, maps and artefacts created in the past – to pursue research and investigation. Warrington is especially fortunate because it has a very rich inheritance of such material, especially for the past three hundred years, and this is readily available to anyone who wants to undertake

In 1848 Warrington created the first public-funded joint museum and library, which moved to its present purpose-built premises in 1857. Today it is the headquarters of Warrington Library, Museum & Archives Service and holds invaluable records for local historians.

research. There is another major advantage: much of the source material is housed in the Museum and the Library, on hand for Warringtonians and easily accessible for people from outside the town and borough. There are three major collections to consider.

WARRINGTON MUSEUM

Warrington Museum is a treasury of the town's history and is itself of major historical importance. Its collections were developed, from the mid-nineteenth century, by building upon the material accumulated by some of the town's leading private citizens. They had acquired objects such as antiquarian curiosities, Roman finds from Wilderspool and natural history specimens during the eighteenth and early nineteenth centuries. In 1811 some of the leading gentlemen of the town formed the grandly titled Institute for the Cultivation of Sciences, Literature and the Arts, which included a small private museum. In 1838 the Natural History Society was formed, and it took over the collections of the Institution and also of the older Warrington Circulating Library, established in 1760. Together, these collections were made available to the wider public, at first informally but from 1848 as the heart of the new Warrington Library and Museum.

Booth's watercolour portrays an idealized rural scene at Warrington Bridge in the 1830s. Industry had yet to crowd the banks of the Mersey and countrywomen could complete their washing in the shadow of Harrison's wooden bridge.

Warrington Library, Museum & Archives Service's photographic collection shows the reality of local life. This view of Warrington Bridge in the 1930s is full of clues for local historians. Street scenes can be dated from road vehicles, how people are dressed and the occupants of shops can be traced through trade directories.

Today the Museum not only houses a superb collection of material relating to the town and its surrounding areas, but also includes a major collection of photographs and other visual material, as well as maintaining permanent and temporary exhibitions and displays which are a showcase for Warrington history past and present. Among the highlights we might include the fine collection of finds from prehistoric sits in the vicinity and from Roman Wilderspool and the paintings and drawings in the art gallery which give us a unique visual record of changing Warrington as seen through the eyes of artists over the past 300 years.

LOCAL STUDIES COLLECTION

The local studies collection in the library is the second major resource available to researchers. Here, too, the work of eighteenth- and nineteenth-century private collectors was invaluable, but since 1848 the library has maintained a careful policy of acquiring all published and printed works relating to Warrington and many of the parishes in the adjacent districts. It has some special collections, such as those concerning Lewis Carroll (because of his close connections with nearby Daresbury) but the general collection of printed works, on all manner of themes and topics, is outstanding.

The local studies collection also includes a very large and comprehensive range of Ordnance Survey maps, covering the past 160 years. If you want to try to locate someone who you think lived in a particular place in the nineteenth century or first half of the twentieth it is worth checking the local street and trade directories. These are reasonably comprehensive, and arranged street by street and house by house, from the late nineteenth century onwards. Before then, they usually only include the tradesmen, retailers and others engaged in commerce and business, together with the citizens of higher social status. They are very useful for finding an address which can be cross-referenced with the nearest census returns.

Local newspapers can be a valuable source for family historians, though they are not easy to use. Most papers, from the early nineteenth century onwards, included a 'births, marriages and deaths' column, though it was not until the later nineteenth century that these included entries from working-class families – until then it was usually only people higher up the social scale who publicized family events in this way. Newspapers also give plenty of information about specific events and can be especially useful if, for example, someone in your family met with a tragic end – reports of sudden and violent deaths, and detailed accounts of the coroner's inquest, may well be found. The main problem with using local papers is that you may need to search through hundreds of pages – there are very few adequate indexes.

Professional and amateur photographers have recorded the changing face of Warrington and its inhabitants since the mid-1850s. Thomas Birtles (seen here) headed a studio which documented street scenes, captured news events and produced portraits in an era before instant digital snaps and the immediacy of images transmitted from camera phones.

William Beamont, Warrington's first mayor, was one of the town's most prolific local historians. He collated records from estate papers and medieval documents, and his own political career can be traced in the minutes of Warrington Borough Council Committees.

Warrington Library holds microfilm copies of most local papers from the mid-nineteenth century onwards (notably, the *Warrington Guardian* continuously from 1853 to 2004), but because of the high demand for the use of microfilm readers booking in advance is essential.

A further part of the local studies collection which is of outstanding value is its excellent photographic collection. The local studies room is at the back of the reference library, to the right of the enquiries desk.

ARCHIVE COLLECTION

The third resource is the archive collection, which is also available in the local studies room. Archives are almost always unique and irreplaceable manuscript and documentary material, rather than printed works and for reasons of security the material is housed in the strongrooms 'behind the scenes' so researchers need to ask to see items. There are many catalogues and explanatory leaflets are also available and staff on hand to assist you with locating and ordering documents and other items from the collections. As with the Museum and Library collections, some of the archives were acquired by local

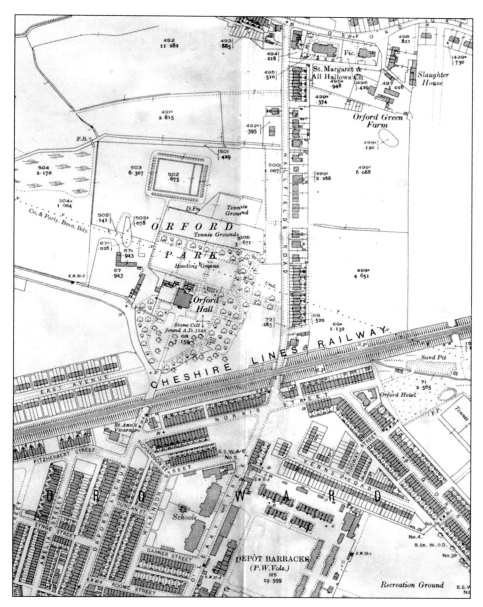

Maps are invaluable to anyone interested in local history. This Ordnance Survey extract shows historic Orford Hall and its surroundings. Compare this with earlier and later maps housed in the library's local studies section to see how the district changed in time. Trace the inhabitants of your house or an ancestor via census returns or trade directories.

historians and antiquarians in the eighteenth and nineteenth centuries, but after 1848 successive borough librarians continued to add to the collection. Among the particular strengths of the borough collections are the superb Georgian and Victorian records relating to the Poor Law and public health; the borough's own records (the archives of the Police Commissioners, the Corporation and the Borough Council since the early nineteenth century); the papers, including diaries and journals, of some of the leading figures of Victorian Warrington, such as William Beamont of Orford Hall; papers relating to the other (once-rural) townships which now form part of the borough; and the records of many of the major industrial and commercial firms which helped to shape the town and the lives of its people, such as Greenalls. Yet the archives are not only about officials, local government, big businesses and the local elite. They also contain numerous small collections – sometimes only single documents – which relate to ordinary people, private citizens, small businesses, individual properties and the humdrum and routine realities of everyday life in the past.

Because Warrington was formerly part of the administrative county of Lancashire, and from 1974 to 1998 was within Cheshire (and still is for some purposes) there is also a good deal of relevant archive material elsewhere. For example, the wills of Warringtonians (and of people from other parishes north of the river) from the early sixteenth century onwards are to be found

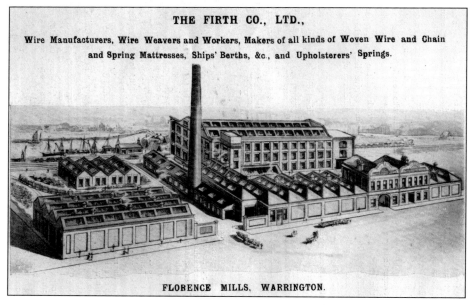

Did one of your relatives work in one of Warrington's wireworks like the Firth Co., seen here in the 1908 Trade Directory? Trace their lives through company archives, local newspapers, trade catalogues, photographs or oral history accounts of former employees.

Who do you think they are? Start with your family records or tape elderly relatives' reminiscences. Use the Library Museum & Archives Service to access census data before 1901, maps and photographs of the area, school records or explore where the parents worked or worshipped. Look for details of births, marriages and deaths in the local newspapers, or church records and log onto the internet to take your quest further

at the Lancashire Record Office in Preston, as are the records of the quarter sessions courts (for the Warrington area these sat at Wigan or Ormskirk and records survive from the late sixteenth century to the twentieth century). The parish records, on the other hand, are to be found at the Cheshire Record Office in Chester, though the local studies collection has microfilm or micro-fiche copies of most of these. This means that family and local historians, or people searching the history of a house or a street, will probably need to visit either or both of the county record offices for certain categories of documentary material.

As well as the printed word and the handwritten or typewritten document there is another key source of historical evidence: the people of Warrington themselves. Of course many people in the past have left us written records, and many others appear in those records, but since the middle of the twentieth century the present-day inhabitants of the borough have provided us with their memories and recollections, giving posterity an account of their personal experiences and their own lives. Oral history, whether in the form of sound recordings or transcripts, gives new and exciting dimensions to history of the community. Here, Joe recalls growing up in the town centre in the 1920s:

> the street was our home; our playground; our life. It was cobbled with a tiled pavement of diamond design which we used for all kinds of games. In the summer the women stood at the front doors and conversations were carried on, passing along the street from door to door and across the street like waves, while the pavements were crowded with us kids playing our street games.

Official records don't tell us what it sounded like, smelled like or felt like to work in a tannery, draw wire, sell fish on the market, be in hospital in the 1950s or any one of countless other everyday and commonplace experiences which have now vanished for ever. Warrington Museum and Library have important collections of oral history, often supported by photographs and sometimes by film, to give us insights into those vanished or fast-disappearing worlds, and they, just as much as the records of councils and churches, companies and courts, or the filtered and sifted and reworked writings of historians, provide us with a sense of what Warrington and its constituent communities were like in the past.

It is important to remember that history is always being made, and that what happens today will be history tomorrow. What seems ordinary and unremarkable to us is going to be of great interest to future generations, so we hope very much that the citizens of early twenty-first-century Warrington will want to capture their memories and experiences in the same way, so that the work of building up a resource for posterity will continue.

CHAPTER THREE

A CHANGING TOWN
CENTRE

The centre of any town is more than just the physical heart of a community. It plays a vital role in all sorts of other ways — as a meeting place;
as a retailing and commercial district; as the location of public buildings and
monuments; as a focus for cultural and civic life; and as a setting for great
occasions and events. A town which lacks a centre is a town which is
diminished and disadvantaged. Warrington is very fortunate, therefore, to
have a centre which has for almost a thousand years helped to define the

*In 1855 Golden Square
was about to undergo the
first of three major
regenerations in 150
years. The old Manor
Court House (centre)
had ceased to be the centre
of administration and
was being demolished to
make way for a new
covered market. This
early photograph reveals
a link to an earlier
important landmark in
the column of dressed
stone which had been
reused from the old
Warrington Friary.*

23

A visitor to late eighteenth-century Warrington described Bridge Street as 'narrow, long, ill-built and crowded with carts and passengers'. This view of 1887 captures the scene at the junction with Mersey Street looking towards the town centre. Over the next twenty years the streetscape would change dramatically as the whole of the west side (left) was demolished and rebuilt.

town's identity. The area around the market place and the nearby crossroads has been the scene of much drama in the past, as well as a focal point in the lives of so many citizens of the town over the centuries. Today, despite the emergence of out-of-town shopping areas and the challenge posed by different patterns of shopping and retailing, the centre of the town remains a major focus of commercial activity.

The original centre of the town was the stretch of Church Street leading eastwards to the gates of the parish church. Here were the first market place, the ancient church, the site of the pre-Conquest fortification and perhaps a short-lived Norman castle. In the thirteenth century this area lost its place at the heart of the growing town as a new focus emerged over half a mile to the west, at the crossroads above the river at the top of the long slope of Bridge Street. Here, where the two great routes from east to west and north to south crossed, a new town centre began to develop. The commercial attractions of the site were as clear then as they are today, for at that location there was the maximum passing trade and greatest accessibility. Within quite a short time a great new market place, a large open rectangle, had been laid out just behind the street frontages of Horsemarket Street and Sankey

Hidden behind the respectable facades of the four main shopping streets were the crowded, dark and insanitary courtyards which had become home to Warrington's rapidly expanding population by the late nineteenth century. Dolman's Lane off Bridge Street (near the site of the present market) was typical of these 'rookeries' of working-class tenants who seemed to have stepped straight from the pages of a novel by Charles Dickens.

Street, very close to the crossroads. The friary was just to the south, on the west side of Bridge Street and close by, five centuries later, two of Warrington's most important religious buildings were constructed: the Cairo Street chapel (1703; rebuilt 1745) and Holy Trinity Church (1709; rebuilt 1760).

It is probable that in the thirteenth century the four main streets were already lined with shops and houses and so the space for the new market place had to be found on the land behind, on what was then agricultural land. Even today, notice how this market place (part of Golden Square) is hidden behind the street frontages and no major thoroughfare passes through it — there are just narrow lanes and entries linking it with the adjacent streets. The market place was deliberately laid out and planned, and its commercial success meant that within a few decades its edges were also lined with new buildings, as merchants and tradesmen came to live and work and trade in this favourable location. Before long the square itself began to be infilled with additional buildings, so that by the early nineteenth century there was

By 1905 the widening of Bridge Street to 60 feet had almost reached Market Gate. To minimize the disruption, new shops had been built behind the older premises which were demolished as each new block was completed. Here Warrington's new tram network is being extended to allow businessmen and shoppers to commute from the new suburbs.

By the 1930s Market Gate was already becoming a bottleneck on the region's major east–west and north–south traffic networks. Bridge Street and Buttermarket Street had already been widened but the widening of Horsemarket Street was not completed for another half-century. Millings and Peter Leigh's grocery stores and their neighbours survived until the building of Golden Square in the 1970s–1980s.

In 1856 Warrington's open air market was replaced by the ornate market hall and attached 'shed'. These were virtually the only survivors of the redevelopment of the market place area and surrounding neighbourhood in the late 1970s–1980s.

A view from inside the Market Hall, looking towards Holy Trinity Church in Sankey Street photographed in the late 1940s. The ornate wrought iron work of George Bowcock's butcher's stall was a reminder of mid-Victorian grandeur in an era where shoppers still struggled to cope with post-Second World War food rationing.

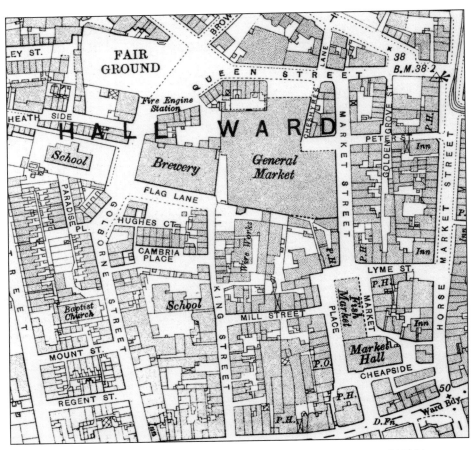

Warrington's old town centre market area (shown here on the OS map of 1900) was already known as Golden Square by 1772. By the 1840s there was a thriving open air market there which was replaced by a covered market hall and attached covered fish market in the mid-1850s. A larger general market was added behind the Barley Mow pub in the 1880s.

a quaint and irregular untidiness of buildings and small open spaces, which would now be regarded as delightful and historic but which offended Victorian notions of neatness and order. In the late 1850s the buildings were cleared away and the rectangular form of the market place once again became apparent. Long before then, though, the new market place was too small for the volume of trade handled, so that stalls had spilled out onto the nearby streets. The names 'Buttermarket' and 'Horsemarket' tell us of the commodities which were traded there in the medieval period and afterwards, a direct link with the commercial vigour of Warrington six centuries ago.

The market clock was ticking away the last hours of the old general market as Harold Critchley captured the bustling atmosphere of the early 1970s. Soon the bulldozers would move in to clear the way for the new Golden Square shops as the whole market complex was relocated to its present site behind Bridge Street.

LIVING IN THE TOWN CENTRE

Until the early nineteenth century Warrington was a very compact town. With the exception of the area around the parish church and along Church Street, almost all the built-up area was along the four main roads leading to Market Gates and most housing was within a quarter of a mile of the market place. Behind the main streets – and especially Bridge Street and Horsemarket Street – stretched the narrow burgage plots, the main property divisions of the medieval town, each with a short street frontage and a long backyard or back garden. As the town began to grow in the later eighteenth century, much of the population increase was accommodated not so much by the development of new housing areas and new suburbs as by infilling and building on the land to the rear the main streets. Such housing was almost invariably of inferior quality, and its occupants were from the outset among the poorest of the townspeople. By the late 1840s the yards and courts behind Bridge Street, Buttermarket Street and Horsemarket Street had become notorious for their poverty and unhealthy environment. These were the areas most badly affected by the devastating cholera epidemic of 1832. It

29

This view from Holy Trinity clock tower shows Buttermarket Street in the 1960s. In the foreground is the old traffic roundabout (now the site of the Well of Light). Two cinemas on the left (the domed Empire and the art deco Odeon further down) are a reminder of earlier town centre night life. In the background are the factories of Cockhedge and Howley.

was here that desperate levels of overcrowding were found. The congested and squalid properties in courts behind Ship Street were the areas where, in the 1850s, the new wave of Irish migrants had little choice but to go, and it was to these insanitary hovels and airless stagnant yards that Warrington's social reformers, such as the Nonconformist minister P P Carpenter, turned their attention in the late 1840s when they strove to raise public awareness of the evils which were hidden immediately behind the facades of the town's main streets.

By the late nineteenth century the worst excesses of deprivation were being ameliorated. Piped water supplies and the provision of a sewerage system made their mark, as did the greater availability of small, but significantly better quality, terraced housing in the newer working-class districts. The gradual extension of the shopping area during the later Victorian period was another key factor, allowing the redevelopment of some of the worst sites, a process which became much more important between the two world wars as slum clearance and rehousing formed a major element of the council's policies. During the last half-century almost all traces of these Victorian

A view up Buttermarket Street, near St Mary's Church, shows the 'Little Red Riding Hoods' leading the 1894 Walking Day procession. The imposing building on the left is the Bridewell and Sessions House in Irlam Street. This was the headquarters of Warrington's expanding police force from 1820 to 1900 and conveniently located next to the town centre's most built-up areas.

'rookeries', notorious in their day for deprivation, social ills, crime and squalor, have disappeared as the town centre and its adjacent areas have been extensively remodelled. The result was that the number of residents in central Warrington fell drastically, to the point where in the late 1980s almost nobody was living in an area which, only two hundred years before, had been the home of more or less the entire population. Now we can only recall the character and appearance of the Victorian courts and yards from haunting contemporary photographs, the detailed Ordnance Survey maps and plans, the vivid descriptions of social reformers and the occasional glimpse of a dark narrow entry or court behind shops or office property.

THE TOWN HALL AND CIVIC LIFE

In the middle years of the eighteenth century, just beyond the edge of the town, a splendid new building arose, a landmark which stood on the flat summit of a low ridge, fronted by green slopes leading down towards the long northwards curve of the Mersey. This was Bank Hall, the seat of the Patten family. Thomas Patten (d. 1726) was the man responsible for the improvements which had made the river navigable for larger vessels up to Warrington Bridge, and was also one of the leading industrialists and

From the mid-1870s the focal point of Warrington's civic life has been its imposing town hall. Built for Thomas Patten it is clearly recognizable on the left of Donbavand's 1772 view of the town centre from the River Mersey. To the extreme right of the scene is Holy Trinity Church and further to its left is the tower of the old Manor Court House in the Market Place.

entrepreneurs in north-west England. His son, another Thomas, carried on the family businesses, which included glass-making, copper-smelting and warehousing and trading in sugar and tobacco. The profits of these many and varied commercial interests allowed him in the years after 1750 to build the new house, conveniently located near to the works and the warehouses, and handy for the town, but still among the fields and with fine views to the river and over into Cheshire.

It was a most imposing building, in the fashionable classical style, with a great three-storey columned front crowned by a sculpted pediment and approached by a grand flight of steps from the lawns which surrounded the house. In Donbavand's endlessly informative picture of Warrington from the south, painted in 1772, Bank Hall still stands proudly, although between it and the town some new houses had sprung up. But this painting fore-shadows the future, for even more prominent in the view than the great house are the two huge cones of the glassworks beside the river at the foot of the slope, smoke pouring from their pointed tops and rivalling, in their visual dominance, the tall and ornamented tower of Holy Trinity church. By the 1860s a multitude of other chimneys belched polluting smoke and fumes into Warrington's skies and, although the front lawns were still there, the long green slopes down to the river had been built over. Trains puffed and rattled past on the main railway line just 150 yards from the house, and the noise and clamour of the town had destroyed the peace and quiet. There were serious suggestions that the building should be demolished and its site given over to housing and industry.

Fortunately, and in retrospect almost miraculously, Warrington

By the 1900s bay-fronted villas had appeared on the fringes of the town centre to house the middle classes. Winmarleigh Street (named after Patten's descendants) encroached on the town hall which is half hidden behind its ornate gates and the bulky Walker Fountain in the background. New technology had arrived in the shape of the tower of masts on Warrington's first telephone exchange and the posts of the electric tram network.

Palmyra Square was crowded in February 1907 to witness the unveiling of the statue of Lt Colonel McCarthy O'Leary and the memorial to Warrington's volunteer soldiers killed in the Boer War. Construction workers on the new Post Office building (background right) had a grandstand view of the occasion.

This 1900s view shows the newly completed county court building and the neighbouring borough gymnasium. Today these have been converted into the Pyramid Arts Centre in Warrington's new Cultural Quarter.

Artist Hamlet Winstanley's portrait shows Thomas Patten as a successful eighteenth-century entrepreneur who could afford to hire world-famous architect James Gibbs to create a brick mansion suitable for a new urban aristocracy. Patten's wealth possibly had a darker side as his copperworks was indirectly linked to the slave trade. Patten's great-grandson (later Lord Winmarleigh) sold it to Warrington Borough Council with 13 acres of land in 1872.

*In the late eighteenth century Warrington
saw itself as a major cultural centre with
the establishment of Warrington
Academy between 1757 and 1786. Its
distinguished tutors included Joseph
Priestley and John Aiken, whose
daughter Anna Laetitia Barbauld also
achieved literary fame. Already a
successful poet she published* Lessons for
Children *and* Hymns in Prose, *two of
the first books written especially for
children, but with a moral slant.*

*Philip Pearsall
Carpenter, minister of
Cairo Street chapel,
became known as
campaigner for public
health reform in the
1850s. Meanwhile, in the
insanitary crowded
courtyards off Bridge
Street, unsung heroine
Hanna Phillips gave
practical help to poor
families and tended their
sick children.*

Corporation intervened. The council had been contemplating the construction of a new town hall, to rival those of the great cotton towns of Lancashire, but was reluctant to spend the money even if it could have found it. The chance to purchase a ready-made building was too tempting to resist, even though the Georgian architecture of Bank Hall was, in the 1860s, regarded as hideous and gross. The deal was done and, not by preference but largely by accident, Warrington found itself a town hall which, 140 years later, is recognized as one of the finest eighteenth-century buildings in the north-west. It is a monument not only to the good taste of the Pattens but also, perhaps, to the parsimony of the Victorian councillors and aldermen who preferred to economize. Thank goodness they did!

THE CULTURAL QUARTER

Some of those gentlemen lived just down the road from Bank Hall, in the fashionable new residential district which was developing from the middle of the nineteenth century in the vicinity of Palmyra Square. This was a relatively small district geographically, but a significant part of the town's growing commercial and industrial wealth was concentrated there. Large terraced and semi-detached houses edged the square itself, which was laid out with private gardens accessible only to the residents. The streets were wide and spacious, the houses had small front gardens and were architect-designed, with dark red brick and stone window surrounds, porches and doorways. The social tone was exclusive and many of the early residents were families who had previously lived in areas such as Church Street, fast deteriorating because of the encroachment of industry. Doctors, lawyers, managers of businesses and owners of companies found the area congenial. On the southern edge of the new residential area the town's cultural aspirations bore fruit in the construction, from 1855 onwards, of the Museum and Library (1855–7), one of the first anywhere in Britain to be purpose-built.

The area has a clear and strong identity of its own. It covers just one square and a few adjacent streets, and very quickly merges north-westwards into the town centre proper, but everywhere the signs of status are apparent. The front gardens, the architectural embellishments, the gateposts and the garden walls all give clues to the social ambitions of the people who built and lived in these streets a century and a half ago. But here, too, deterioration was fairly soon apparent. By the early twentieth century it was noted that houses were being vacated by their residents and turned over to other uses, as surgeries, lawyers' and accountants' offices and private academies. The families were moving 'to the Cheshire side' and commuting to their former homes for work. In the mid-twentieth century there was piecemeal re-development of some sites, while on the fringes of the town centre housing was turned over to multiple uses and experienced rapid decay, a process exemplified by the visual and physical deterioration of the square itself.

At the end of the twentieth century, the district underwent the beginnings of a transformation, rechristened and given a new identity as the Cultural Quarter and enjoying extensive repair and enhancement of its fabric. Appropriate new buildings, the complete revitalization and reconstruction of the square and its gardens, the provision of major new arts facilities including the Pyramid, and the removal of through traffic have restored an attractive townscape and given a peaceful environment, one in which some of Warrington's finest streets can again be appreciated and savoured.

While the historic townscape has been revitalized, a new urban landscape of apartment blocks and regenerated shopping malls is emerging to give a new heart to twenty-first-century Warrington.

CHAPTER FOUR

HOWLEY AND FAIRFIELD

At Howley the original course of the river still follows its series of lazy curves and the riverside, though so many of its industries have vanished, still reminds us of the important part which the waterway played in the development of the area. It is surprisingly easy to forget that the river was fundamental to the location and development of Warrington, and many people are probably hardly aware of its existence. This is partly because there have been so many physical alterations to its course. In the 1720s and 1730s, when the channel was improved as part of the project to make the Mersey and the Irwell navigable from Warrington up to Manchester, a number of short diversions and cut-offs were constructed, and during the rest of the eighteenth century successive improvements to the navigation, such as the

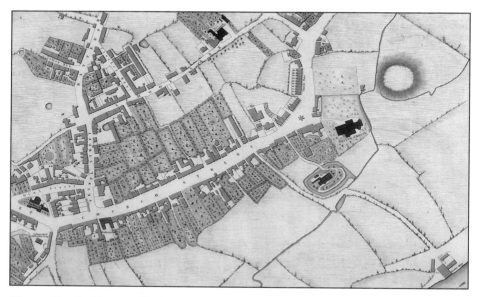

The medieval village of Howley, surrounded by open fields, is still visible on Hall's 1826 map. The remains of the circular mound of the castle (right) stand next to the parish church and its moated rectory near the route to the old ford (Howley Lane). The wide main street, site of annual fairs, is lined with long narrow plots of medieval cottages and gardens and the back lane leads to the grammar school.

The old grammar school, seen here in the early 1900s, was established in 1526 by the will of Sir Thomas Boteler. It educated local boys in Latin, Greek, mathematics and religious instruction. It was rebuilt in the mid-nineteenth century, transferred to a new site at Latchford in 1940 and subsequently became a mixed-sex comprehensive school whilst the old building was eventually demolished.

two-mile Woolston New Cut, altered the original course more drastically. The building of the Manchester Ship Canal had a more far-reaching impact, because it took so much water from the original river and thus led to the shrinking of the old course. At Warrington itself the bridge, rebuilt in 1911–13, is now so wide that many people driving over it do not even realize that it is a bridge.

At the foot of Howley Lane, opposite Victoria Park, there was the crucial ford which was used from prehistoric times until it was superseded by the bridge in the middle of the thirteenth century. Along the riverside were some of the town's chief medieval and later industries, including the water-driven cornmills which supplied Warrington with its flour. The name Howley means 'the marshy meadow [or pasture] in the hollow [or bend] of the river', which would admirably have described its character a thousand years ago, and here, as at Arpley ('the dark meadow'), the people of Warrington had land to graze their cattle and to cut their hay.

At the top of the slope above the river at Howley was the place where Warrington began. Though much altered by recent improvements, the irregular alignment of Howley Lane and the top end of Farrell Street reminds us that this is an ancient route. It led to that very important place where, until the thirteenth century, the parish church, the market place and the castle mound stood side by side, representing the three great pillars of early

St Elphin's (or Elfin's) church at Warrington is recorded in the Domesday Book of 1086, but had probably existed from the seventh century. This 1830s view of Warrington's parish church and adjacent Ring O' Bells pub looks very picturesque but the fabric of the old church was in decay.

Church Street's annual summer fair had taken place since medieval times. In 1900 Robert Davies recalled seeing 'stalls, called standings, swing boats and peep shows on the southerly side of the street . . . and donkey and even horse races were run up Manchester Road'. It was too lively an event for Victorian Warrington and was discontinued in 1859.

medieval society: religion, money and administrative and military power. Though the market moved from there more than seven centuries ago its site can readily be seen, while the magnificent spire of the church of St Elphin, though a Victorian addition, is the crowning glory of a building whose origins go back perhaps 1300 years and which still has substantial parts of its medieval fabric intact. Though the market moved away, Church Street remained the town's most desirable residential area for another five centuries, and this is reflected in the surviving examples of fine black and white architecture. The Marquis of Granby, for example, was originally a town house. The setting of these examples of Warrington's traditional architectural styles was sadly altered by industrialization in the nineteenth century and the collapse of those industries in the twentieth, but at long last the rejuvenation of this ancient and historic part of the town is well under way.

As we have seen, the earliest industry in the area was cornmilling, but from at least the early seventeenth century, and probably well before that, Howley became the centre of Warrington's important tanning trade. The huge numbers of skins and hides which were cured and tanned here provided the leather which was the material for another of the town's major trades, making gloves, harness, hats and footwear. The tanneries were located here partly because it was conveniently close to the markets and slaughterhouses

With Church Street bedecked for the royal visit of Edward VII in July 1909, local children enjoy a school holiday. Doubtless many attended the Parochial National School (opened in 1833) which towers above the white cottage on the left.

41

A small child could safely play on Church Street's pavements in the early 1900s. Only two landmarks remain today: the parish church with its spire (right) and the black and white cottage (left). Rylands wireworks (far left), Warrington Training College (in the far distance), terraced cottages, gas lamps and cobblestones are all long vanished.

Built beside the parish church in 1844 to house the Clergy Daughters' School, these gothic premises were later shared by Warrington's Teacher Training College. The school moved to Darley Dale in 1907 and the college was gutted by a devastating fire on 28 December 1923. Today only St Katherine's Chapel survives as a community centre.

– Horsemarket Street and the butcher's shambles of the market place were only just up the road – and partly because tanning required large quantities of water, which was mixed with lime in pits so that the skins could be steeped in the corrosive alkaline solution. This softened and rotted the fat, flesh, and hair or bristle, which could then be scraped away with great knives. The resultant stinking effluent could then be released into drains and ditches and returned to the unfortunate Mersey. By the mid-nineteenth century there were several tanneries in the vicinity of Mersey Street and Hall Street, and in 1863 the great Central Tanneries by the river were opened (they lasted until 1960). Other major industries had appeared in Howley by that time. In the late eighteenth century wire-working, formerly a small domestic trade, had started to grow in scale and significance, as the demands of industry and agriculture expanded. John Rylands and Nathaniel Greening opened their Church Street works in 1817 and seventy years later there were more than 1,000 men employed there. The works had spread to gobble up nearby sites and by 1905 it extended, with only the main road and the grammar school in the way, as far as the Cheshire Lines Railway.

These industries, and the geographical location, gave Howley and its 'suburb' of Fairfield an almost self-contained character, cut off by the river, the town centre and the railway and with a strong identity of its own, with

Fairfield Hall off Manchester Road was built for Anna Blackburne of Orford Hall. She was a noted botanist and ornithologist in her own right, with a new species of plant and bird named after her. After her father's death she set up her own residence at Fairfield, complete with natural history gallery. On her death in 1793 the hall became a private school before being rented by Warrington Training College.

43

A view of Ryland's wireworks in Church Street about 1980, taken from the parish church spire. Together with Lockers and the Firth Co. Rylands had made the wire industry a major employer in Howley. The works were demolished in 1983 and soon the only wire seen on the site was that in Sainsbury's supermarket trolleys!

Riverside industries at Howley Quay, pictured in the mid-1960s.

Residents of Dutton Street, Howley, put on a display of community spirit to celebrate the Silver Jubilee of King George V in 1935.

By the late 1970s the face of Church Street changed dramatically to accommodate the growing volume of traffic. The Co-operative store (right) and neighbouring premises made way for the new Mersey Street traffic island.

Reverend William Quekett (pictured here with his redoubtable wife Louisa) became rector of Warrington in 1854. He was shocked at the poverty of the town and its crumbling parish church, which he set about rebuilding between 1857 and 1869. His triumph was fundraising for the 281 foot great spire, the third highest in the country and achieved by his effective campaign slogan of 'a guinea for a golden cock'.

Many Howley residents profited from an illegal bet on champion local jockey Steve Donaghue! Seen here, celebrating his sixth Derby victory in 1925 at a party he threw for local schoolchildren, he never forgot his links with St Mary's School. Born in Warrington in 1884, he seemed destined for a steelworks but seized a chance to become a jockey, in an illustrious career that saw 2,000 victories.

Few of Howley's residents became famous, but all contributed to its history. These women employees of Chadwick's paper mill recalled working long hours for poor pay and without trade union protection. One Chadwick's employee later remarked, 'I don't know whether I was more happy at leaving work than getting married!'

its tightly packed terraced streets and a community cemented together by the fact that so many of its men worked in the two key industries. The loss of those industries, and the large-scale redevelopment of the 1960s to the 1980s, including the construction of the Mersey Street dual carriageway, had the effect of fragmenting the community. The great Rylands works on Church Street was perhaps the most important single change, but all across the area there was a major loss of people and employment. Some observers more or less wrote off Howley, regarding it as a district with no future and suggesting that new light industry should replace almost all the residential areas. But Howley residents are proud of their area's past and many were determined not only that the community should not die but that its history should be recorded and remembered. This is reflected in the work of the Howley Heritage Group in showing, with a heritage trail among other projects, how much history still remains. No less important is the future, for the revival of Howley is now in progress. Though we might regret that so much of historical interest has been lost, the creation of a new community is a key element in plans for the future of the area where Warrington began and which still contains some of its most historic buildings.

CHAPTER FIVE

LATCHFORD, WESTY AND THE LOUSHERS LANE ESTATE

What's in a name? In Latchford's case, everything, as its name originated from its function as a 'ford' or crossing over a 'laecc', meaning a boggy place or stream. The thoroughfare down present-day Wash Lane marked the place where earliest travellers found the River Mersey shallow enough to be crossed on foot or by cart from the Cheshire side to Howley. Evidence of Bronze Age settlement in the Euclid Avenue area of Grappenhall can be traced back over 4,000 years to what was then a spot on high ground near to the ford.

In Roman times Latchford was on the fringes of the main industrial settlement at Wilderspool but during the construction of the Loushers Lane estate in the early 1930s the discovery of the remains of a building with a hypocaust (or Roman under-floor central heating) suggested that there was an important ancillary settlement in the area. It is more than likely that the Romans would have continued to use the established route across the ford as well as their own more sophisticated road.

Latchford is not named in the Domesday Book of 1086 as it was then still a part of Grappenhall, long before the modern industrial canal network cut it adrift. In the period following the Norman Conquest Warrington's centre of gravity switched to the Howley side of the ford as the Boteler barons built their castle in Church Street. Latchford was not to be outdone: by the reign of Richard I it was the focus for a rival dynasty, the Boydell family, and found itself at the centre of an early example of road rage.

Hugh de Boydell was given the right to charge tolls on travellers crossing the Mersey at Latchford. This became an increasingly lucrative concession as the Botelers' ambitions grew. Traders heading to the Botelers' new market in Church Street found they had to pay the Boydells' toll to reach it. The Botelers retaliated by 1285 and provided an alternative river crossing in the shape of Warrington Bridge for which they collected tolls. The Boydell family were not prepared to suffer this threat to their power and wealth and were alleged to have prevented travellers from Cheshire reaching the new bridge by blocking access to a vital road junction in Latchford of present-

Built for Richard Warburton in 1656 this half-timbered house in Wash Lane achieved notoriety as the 'Plague House'. The missing coping stone on the lower right-hand corner of the wall can now be seen in Warrington Museum. The stone has a small hollow which would be filled with vinegar to disinfect coins left by the infected householders in return for food.

day Thelwall Lane, Knutsford Road and Grappenhall Road. The dispute dragged on until the mid-fifteenth century when the Earl of Derby replaced Warrington Bridge at his own expense and effectively ended the tolls by financing the upkeep of the bridge himself.

Latchford itself was still relatively uninhabited at this time but a survey of 1466 for the Legh family does provide an early reference to the Ackers Lane area. William Murray was renting from Peter Legh

> one parcel of land containing an acre or more . . . enclosed with hedges and ditches called le akkirs which parcel lies in breadth between the arable land of the said Peter on the east and part of Lacheforthe Heath on the west and extends in length from a certain lane leading from Lacheforthe towards the township of Knottisforthe on the south.

By the mid-seventeenth century records of early Latchford households appear, most notably Richard Warburton's house in Wash Lane. This large half-timbered house achived notoriety as the Plague House, where tradition stated that several of its occupants were struck down by one of the deadly outbreaks of the contagious disease which culminated in the Great Plague of 1666. The exact date of the Latchford plague is uncertain but credence was given to the story in the mid-nineteenth century when human remains were found behind the house, evidently hastily buried in unconsecrated ground without even a coffin. The distance to the nearest churchyard at St Wilfrid's Grappenhall probably explained the unceremonious burial and another century passed before Latchford had its own church with the building of the original St James's Church off Knutsford Road in 1777.

By 1801 the face of Latchford was beginning to change dramatically. Improvements to the navigation of the River Mersey itself saw the site of the old ford disappear, whilst the opening of the Old Quay Canal that year effectively bisected the area. The area of Latchford nearest to Warrington Bridge became increasingly industrialized. In 1787 the first Boulton and Watt steam engine to be installed in a Lancashire cotton factory came to Peel Ainsworth's mill, and Edelsten's pin works was employing young children. Between the Censuses of 1801 and 1831 Latchford's population grew from 754 to 2,166, largely as a result of this industrialization. By the

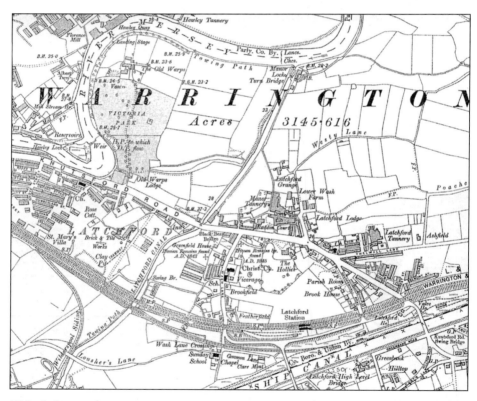

This Ordnance Survey map shows the development of Latchford village by the early twentieth century. The Manchester Ship Canal had cut Latchford off from Grappenhall whilst the earlier Latchford (or Black Bear) Canal had divided the village in two. The town end of Knutsford Road was crowded with housing whilst the Westy and Loushers Lane council estates had yet to appear in the open fields around Latchford village.

In the early eighteenth century the course of the River Mersey through Latchford was altered by the construction of a weir and locks to enable boats to sail up river from Bank Quay. The site of ancient ford disappeared with the alteration of loop of the river near Howley. This early twentieth-century photograph shows the Old Warps estate in the background.

A view of Manor Lock which enabled boats to reach the Mersey near Howley from the Old Quay Canal (also known as the Latchford or Black Bear Canal).

The Hollies on Knutsford Road was the home of Charles Broadbent, local Conservative politician and owner of the Latchford Tanning Co. in Thelwall Lane. After his death in 1887 his widow and daughters established themselves as ladies of the manor of Latchford and patrons of Christ Church in Wash Lane. The Hollies was demolished for a road-widening scheme in the mid-1950s.

mid-nineteenth century Latchford also had a link to the regional railway network whilst the building of the Manchester Ship Canal in the early 1890s finally separated from Cheshire.

Meanwhile the tanning industry had come to Latchford village, establishing the Broadbent and Reynolds dynasties with tanneries in Thelwall Lane and at Raddon Court, later followed by Pierpoint and Bryants and Parkinson's Manor Tannery. Latchford had become a suburb of Warrington and a number of large houses appeared to house these prosperous businessmen and local politicians, with the Broadbents at the Hollies and the Reynolds at Raddon Court. Even William Beamont, Warrington's first mayor, took up residence in Rock Villa for a time and later produced a detailed history of the Township of Latchford.

Perhaps in a sign of changing times it was the Broadbent sisters from the Hollies who became the new ladies of the manor, notably the oldest daughter Constance who became Warrington's first lady councillor in 1925. As fascists and socialists grew nearer to open warfare on the international stage she was equally alarmed by the changes on her doorstep. In an article for a local newspaper in 1933 she recalled:

> I have seen enormous changes in Latchford since I was a child, for in
> those days it was a pretty country village. We still speak of it as the

Almost opposite the Hollies stood Raddon Court, built by Sylvanus Reynolds in 1883 as his neighbouring tannery prospered. After his death in a shooting accident in 1887 the house eventually came to be owned by fellow Conservatives, the Greenalls of Walton. In 1914 Raddon Court became a Red Cross Hospital for injured soldiers and supervised by the Broadbent sisters.

Daffodil Day at the Hollies was an annual opportunity for the Broadbent sisters to throw open their gardens for the enjoyment of the villagers and raise funds for one of their many charities.

Village, and it gives us a nasty shock when people say 'What a wonderful garden you have got for the middle of the town.' I can remember when the road to Warrington was of cobble stones. It was frequently flooded and almost impassible. An old Latchfordian, still happily with us, can remember the road being so lonely that she was not allowed to walk into Warrington herself.

Up Westy, as it used to be called, now a populous suburb, were delightful meadows, full of wild flowers . . . foget-me-nots, May flowers, roses, marsh marigolds. Grappenhall Road, Latchford was a pretty lane, the hedges full of woodbine and carpeted with violets.

Constance Broadbent was chiefly alarmed by the influx of council tenants on her doorstep – so worried in fact that she was one of the supporters of the new St Margaret's Mission created by Christ Church to help ensure that these new heathens would know Christian values.

During the 1920s Warrington Borough Council began to implement the new national housing legislation to provide 'homes fit for heroes' for the troops returning from the horrors of the First World War. Poor housing conditions had been identified as a primary reason for the difficulties in recruiting healthy soldiers to send to the front line. As private landlords had not provided good-quality housing for the working classes local councils were given new responsibilities, funded by government loans. Warrington Borough Council swiftly adopted the policy and chose areas of Latchford for

This postcard view of Latchford Village by local photographer Tonge shows the important junction of three main roads: to the left is Thelwall Lane, in the centre the road to Knutsford and on the right the road to Grappenhall (later called Grammar School Road).

Between 1890 and 1894 the cutting of 'the Big Ditch' or Manchester Ship Canal made a dramatic impact on the Latchford landscape, cutting it off from neighbouring Grappenhall. Here the new high-level railway bridge can be seen in the distance.

These Edwardian skaters would still have regarded themselves as Latchford villagers. Before the cutting of the Ship Canal Ackers Lane itself had run from Wash Lane to Chester Road and Hunts Lane.

This early 1900s view of the new Latchford swing bridge shows an eerie absence of traffic and the new villas for the affluent middle class springing up on the Cheshire side of the Ship Canal.

some of the early estates of the 1920s and 1930s. Thelwall Lane, Westy and Loushers Lane all became the site of council housing estates, with a new road infrastructure to support the new suburbs. The story for each estate was similar: the acquisition of suitable land; the issuing of tenders to local builders to produce almost identical houses based on government specifications and the later provision of shops and bus routes to replace Latchford's old tram route.

The Minutes of Warrington Borough Council's Housing Committee tell the official story of the Loushers Lane estate which was built to provide good-quality rented housing. The total cost of building the houses was £80,508, which was borrowed from the Ministry of Health. In December 1919 the town clerk was first asked to investigate the purchase of land in the Loushers Lane area. The borough surveyor then submitted plans in February 1930 for the development of roads in and across Loushers Lane and Wash Lane. (These would later cost £11,032.) In June 1930 the Minutes record

> Resolved that the authority be given for the purchase from Greenall Whitley & Co Ltd. of approx 33.652 acres (in Loushers Lane) for the sum of £8,850.

The tenders for building the estate are recorded in 1930–1. Local builder Daniel Cooper had the job of erecting: 32 'B3 Type' houses with parlours at £468 each and 184 'A3 Type' houses with kitchens only at £318 each. His nephew Fred Cooper later recalled building the houses:

The Baskerville *is towed from Latchford locks in 1958 at a time when the Ship Canal was still a major transport highway. On the left of the locks is Richmonds foundry which produced the famous 'New World' gas cookers and was a major local employer.*

On 5 July 1907 the foundation stone of Latchford's new council school was laid to house the village's growing numbers of children. It was named after William Bolton, a local businessman and town councillor who became the alderman for Latchford ward in 1884.

Rural Latchford in the early 1900s, where Westy Lane met Lower Wash Lane (later known as Grange Avenue). New terraced housing is already appearing at the junction with Reynolds Street and by the 1930s the old name of Westy had been adopted for the new council estate.

As Warrington Borough Council planned new housing in the Latchford area, a second crossing of the River Mersey was needed to link Manchester Road with Knutsford Road. Construction of the new Kingsway Bridge was completed in 1933, with an official royal opening the following year.

I started work as an apprentice bricklayer in 1931 on the Westy Lane Estate and later worked on Loushers Lane Estate in 1932. My wages were ten shillings (50p) a week supplemented by about another ten shillings from tips when I acted as can lad. It would take about a month to build each pair of houses. The builder, my uncle Dan Cooper had a motto: 'Always have the stuff waiting for the men, never have the men waiting for the stuff,' so the building materials were always to hand.

The houses on Loushers were built with oven ranges and one of my jobs was to clean the steel parts which had a red coating using paraffin. Since it was winter time my fingers were freezing. I hated that job!

In the 1930s–1950s the Loushers Lane area seemed like an island, cut off from nearby Latchford as members of the Loushers Lane Memories Group would later recall. There were rumours that, owing to a builder's error, the estate had been built facing entirely in the wrong direction as it had been intended that Pearson Avenue should have fronted the Ship Canal! Some of the first residents in Clarke Avenue found themselves having to negotiate a huge building site to reach their homes.

At first there were no proper shops, merely 'The Hut' at the top of Wash Lane (later a chip shop). Here Percy Hill provided newspapers, tobacco and sweets and Miss Cook sold groceries. Further afield there was old Mrs Morgan's greengrocery on the corner of Knutsford Road and Wash Lane

In 1930 work began on marking out the roads for the new Loushers Lane housing estate. This view towards Greenall's brewery in the background shows the open fields which had been acquired by the council with a government loan. Council Minutes of 10 August 1906 recorded 'that the new road leading from Wilderspool to the bridge over the Runcorn and Latchford Canal be called Loushers Lane'.

with its gloomy gaslit interior. Fresh bread was delivered by the Co-op van man and his horse and Old Lizzie came round with her horse and cart selling greengrocery door to door. Farmer Brown delivered the milk straight from his cows at nearby Lamb Farm or else the local children went with jugs to collect it – provided they were not frightened away by old Mrs Brown! Joseph Richardson brought the coal from Hall Farm by the crossing at Wash Lane with his horses Ginger and Jess. Within a few years the two shops in Loushers Lane were built and Percy Hill moved there to run the post office and newsagents with his neighbour Cissie Cooper supplying groceries.

Other errands might mean a long walk to catch the bus to town along Knutsford Road or a trek down the gravel path that was then Loushers Lane to Wilderspool Causeway and then on into Stockton Heath. Or there was always the adventure of catching a train at Latchford Station for the trip to Arpley Station near Bridge Foot.

For the children of the estate school meant either a walk to Knutsford Road to Bolton Council School or St Augustine's. Some had an even longer

John Holt recalls moving to Pearson Avenue in the new Loushers Lane estate in 1932:
> *'My first sight of the estate was from the crossbar of my father's bicycle at the age of six and a half. Loushers Lane was an idyllic area to grow up in with open spaces to explore, fields and avenues to play in safely with new playmates and friends.'*

walk to Stockton Heath because Bolton Council School was soon bursting at the seams with the arrival of children from the new estates at Westy and Loushers Lane.

At Loushers Lane the children soon formed their own gangs from each street, with rival Maypoles, and only coming together to do battle with snowballs! Childhood seemed idyllic for they had plenty of open country nearby. There were the delights of the Little Willows and the Big Willows and further away off China Lane was the Buttercup Field, complete with a pond for frog spawning and three deep wells to avoid. In hot weather some went swimming in Duke's canal (the Bridgewater) whilst others took a picnic of sandwiches wrapped in greaseproof paper and a bottle of pop to spend the day at Appleton Dingle.

The Second World War brought new friends with the arrival of GIs from the American base at Burtonwood to their nearby tip. A packet of chewing gum was usually forthcoming whilst the American 'Liberty Boats' sailing up the Manchester Ship Canal brought fresh treasures. The boats were so wide that it seemed the crew had only to lean out and toss oranges or tins of peaches into the eager little hands on the canal bank in the days when everything was strictly rationed. The Americans also brought 'Chuck's Club', a pavilion at the back of what later became Woolacombe Close.

The post-war period brought many changes to the Loushers Lane. The estate got its own bus, a double decker which at first had to be routed down Pearson Avenue, until Loushers Lane was resurfaced and the bridge was strengthened. A few private cars began to appear, although special permission had to be sought for a garage. Familiar landmarks began to disappear, as early resident John Holt recalls:

Gradually the open spaces where we had played as children were covered up by new properties as the population of Warrington increased. Firstly the police houses were built in the field from the Railway Cottage, closing the lower railway. Woolacombe Close was built which covered Richardson's field and the field where Santarone's Club was. More private housing was built at the top of Secker Avenue together with a pair of semi-detached houses in Loushers Lane. The Band Hut used by Martial Arts and the Girl Guides was built where the flat-topped brick air raid shelter had been. The Police Ground was closed and two houses tenanted by policemen were demolished to give access for the building of Minerva Close. Clarke Avenue was extended right along the Manchester Ship Canal bank to Archer Avenue. Flats and other property were built in Archer Avenue where an open field and the Blue Triangle Tennis Club had been situated.

Hall Farm, owned by the Richardson family, and Lamb Farm, owned by Browns, have been demolished. Semi-detached houses have been built on the right-hand side of Wash Lane (coming from

Knutsford Road) and also Our Lady's School behind these new houses. The Plague House has been demolished and a pair of semi-detached housed built on the site. Loushers Lane Post Office has closed. The old lower Latchford railway station and the cottages were demolished and a timber yard replaced them. The upper railway station was demolished and became the site of a garden centre.

In all this change there have been three constant items in the Loushers Lane area: The Baptist Chapel, The Chip Shop and the Football Field opposite the front of the Baptist Chapel. Other places have adapted.

LATCHFORD CHARACTERS

In his day Old Billy was as popular as Red Rum and he was probably the only Warrington character to appear in a *Guinness Book of Records*. He was bred by Edward Robinson of Wild Grave Farm, Woolston, near Warrington. Most of the horse's active life was spent working for the Mersey and Irwell Navigation Co. on the Old Quay Canal. He spent many years towing the canal barges against the current of the River Mersey between Warrington

One of Latchford's most famous residents was Old Billy, the longest lived horse in the world who spent his retirement on the Old Warps estate.

Latchford-born songbird Edna Savage became a popstar in the 1950s and here in 1956 the Mayor and Mayoress of Warrington join in her twenty-first birthday celebrations.

and Manchester. Later he worked as a 'gin horse', helping to raise or lower the loads from the boats by powering the 'gin' or hoist on the canal bank.

In 1819 Old Billy was retired onto a farm at Latchford with a special servant to look after him. He was painted by several artists and was even pulled through the streets of Manchester on a cart to celebrate the coronation of King William IV! He died on 27 November 1822 but his head was stuffed and he later became one of the most popular exhibits at Bedford Museum.

CHAPTER SIX

THE ORFORD AREA

On William Yates's map of Lancashire in 1786 Orford is shown as a scattered community in the rural landscape north-east of the town of Warrington. The map marks Long Lane and Sandy Lane, winding through the countryside. They still wind to this day, betraying their ancient origins and contrasting with the neat geometry of the estate roads on either side. South-west of Orford Green the map marks Orford Hall, labelling it as the residence of J Blackburne Esquire, and south of the hall a double avenue of trees extends towards the town along the line of what is now Battersby Lane, providing a rather grand approach for visitors who might be coming to the house from the Warrington direction.

The Blackburnes had lived at Orford since the early seventeenth century and were among the most prominent landowners and magistrates in the

Orford Hall, the heart of Orford village, is pictured here after its rebuilding by Jonathan Blackburne.

John Blackburne (1693–1786) was responsible for the creation of the hall's gardens bringing new and exotic plants to Orford, including pineapple, sugar cane and cotton. This splendid cedar of Lebanon, one of the first to be planted in this country, was destroyed by a hurricane in February 1868.

Warrington area. The hall itself had been largely rebuilt by Jonathan Blackburne, who was high sheriff of Lancashire and who died in 1724. The house was plain and three-storeyed, with a datestone marked '1716' over the main entrance. During the eighteenth century the family extended the house and acquired new lands, with John Blackburne (1693–1786) particularly notable as an enthusiastic gardener, who laid out the grounds with greenhouses and collections of plants.

Towards the end of the century, though, the family ceased to live at Orford, preferring the seclusion of their other great house, Hale Hall on the Mersey, and Orford Hall was let to a succession of tenants. The census returns tell us something about the mid-Victorian families and their lifestyles, for though the owners were no longer there the occupiers were people of wealth and status. In 1851, for instance, there was a strange household there: four unmarried brothers and sisters who were attended to by five servants (not such a bad ratio, perhaps).

Shortly after this time the lease on the house was acquired by one of Warrington's most important figures, a man of major influence in the town for much of the nineteenth century. This was William Beamont, the attorney and solicitor, who had been born in the house on the market place next to

65

The Orford Obelisk, seen here in the 1860s at Conies Corner (now Orford Lane), had originally been built on high ground near the hall to mark John Blackburne's long life. The inscription read, 'Died at Orford hall, 20 December 1786, aged 93 years. Benefactor of Orford; a Great Botanist; a Christian Gentleman who looked through Nature up to Nature's God.'

A group of early residents of Orford Hall, pictured in the mid-1860s, were possibly the Litton family of Bank Quay Flour Mill or even William Beamont's household.

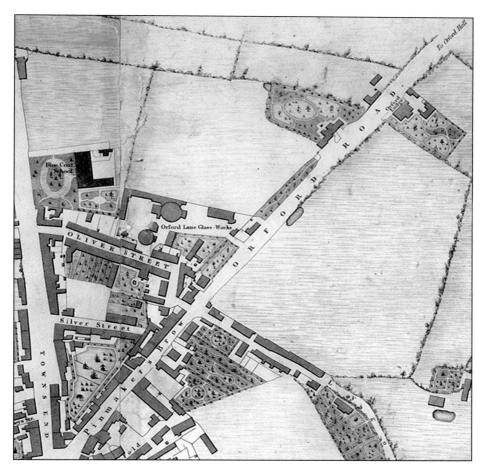

Hall's map of 1826 shows the industrial area which had grown up at the Townsend of Orford Lane. Here were the workshops of pinmakers at Pinners Brow and the Orford Lane Glassworks which later became the site of the Alliance Box Works.

the Barley Mow and had gone on to become the leader of the campaign to secure a charter in the 1840s, and the first mayor of the new borough of Warrington in 1847–8. He was a very prominent historian, passionately interested in his home town and its rich and yet increasingly threatened history. Beamont actively promoted the cultural life of the town, published several books on antiquarian subjects (and especially on his beloved Warrington) and was also very widely known and respected in historical circles throughout north-west England. He loved his life as a country gentlemen and antiquarian: in 1878 he wrote to a friend that, had he to be a full-time practising lawyer, he would have been severely bored, but that because of 'some of the tastes which old deeds and musty parchments, the aroma of age, have left me . . . time never hangs heavy upon me and the

Orford Hall and its residents and staff: 1871 census returns

Residence	Name	Status in household	Condition	Age	Occupation	Birthplace
Orford Hall	William Beamont	head	married	73	landowner	Warrington
	Letitia Beamont	wife	married	60		Liverpool
	Margaret Davies	servant	unmarried	40	domestic servant	Conway
	Frances Wright	servant	unmarried	29	domestic servant	Warrington
	Jane Kelly	servant	unmarried	30	domestic servant	Liverpool
	Martha Hesford	servant	unmarried	19	domestic servant	Grappenhall
Orford	Thomas Jepson	head	married	46	gardener	Fearnhead
	Samuel Jepson	son		14	scholar	Orford
	William Jepson	son		12	scholar	Orford
	Thomas Jepson	son		10	scholar	Orford
	Henry Jepson	son		5	scholar	Orford
Orford	Thomas Booth	head	married	33	coachman	Latchford
	Mary Booth	wife	married	30		Middlewich
	Thomas Booth	son		4	scholar	Orford
	Mary Booth	son		2		Orford
	Joseph Booth	son		9 mths		Orford

longest day seems too short'. It was an idyllic life, albeit in a location which was increasingly overshadowed by industry, but the gentle enjoyment was undoubtedly helped by a complete lack of domestic duties, for in the 1871 census Beamont and his wife, Letitia, are listed as living at Orford Hall with four resident servants (an even better ratio) and with a full-time gardener and a coachman and their families in cottages at the entrance to the park at the western end of Orford Green.

On Beamont's death in 1889 the house was again let, but this time to the Warrington Training College, and it became very badly neglected. In 1907 it was said to stand 'amid the wreckage of what was once a well laid-out and planted garden, with a little wood behind it and a small stream [but] the smoke has killed all the trees and defaced the garden [and] the stream is foul'. By this time the previously rural hamlet was beginning to feel the impact of the town of Warrington. As the census shows, even in the early 1870s many of the inhabitants of Orford no longer worked on the land but were employed in industry. For example, there was a large tannery on Sandy Lane (roughly where Byron Crescent and Morgan Avenue are today) and this employed many local men. In the village there were also men who worked in the glass-works at Orford Lane, in the ironworks at Marsh House Lane, and as fustian-cutters in the loft-like premises on the northern edge of the town centre. The Cheshire Lines Railway had been opened in 1873 passing along the very edge of the hall grounds, greatly diminishing its sense of tranquil-lity and peace. Like so many other rural communities in the Warrington area, the village could not stave off the impact of industrialization for ever, and the old ways were beginning to change by the 1870s and 1880s.

After the First World War the pace of change accelerated. Until 1933 much of Orford, though it was within the parish of Warrington and was part of the parliamentary borough for electoral purposes, was not within the

The Orford Lane Glassworks was the Robinson family's first major enterprise in Warrington until the opening of their better known site at Bank Quay in 1869. Orford Lane continued to produce flint glass under Edward Bolton's control until 1892.

69

After the death of William Beamont's widow in 1902, Orford hall had an uncertain future. Eventually Warrington Borough Council acquired the decaying hall with its extensive grounds. Orford Park opened to the public in 1924 but ten years later the hall itself was demolished.

county borough. For local government functions the northern two-thirds of Orford had been amalgamated with the township of Winwick in 1894. This might not seem to be of much significance, but in fact it was crucial, for as long as it remained outside the control of Warrington the Orford area stood more chance of remaining at least partly rural. In 1933, however, Warrington Corporation (the borough council) secured a private Act of Parliament which authorized the extension of the borough boundaries to include not only the whole of the rest of Orford, but also most of Winwick, Hulme and Great Sankey. Its aim was very clear. The council wanted to build a new ring road to carry traffic out of the town centre, on a route extending from Winwick Road to Knutsford Road, and it wanted to acquire extensive lands on which to develop new municipal housing estates.

As soon as Orford had been brought within the borough, the plans for the new road and the development of the area for housing were implemented. To save money, the council did not choose a completely new and carefully planned alignment for the ring road but instead, where possible, made use of existing roads which were widened but not straightened. Thus, an old country byway, Long Lane and Orford Green, was transformed into a ring road but still with its sharp bends and indirect route. New council and private housing estates spread like a tide across the fields of Orford, on both sides of the 'new but old' road, and Orford Hall, which had become derelict, was demolished and the council landscaped out its grounds as Orford Park. Private developers were also interested in these fields and farms that were ripe for building: in 1938 Charles Forsyth, a local builder, could advertise his 'modern labour-saving houses' in Marina Drive for a deposit of the princely sum of £10 and a purchase price of £435. For that, the lucky buyer would acquire a detached three-bedroomed house with tiled kitchenette, and even (a sure sign of the modern age) a garage.

Today it is quite hard to imagine that Orford, so busy and so full of

New private housing was developed at Orford in 1935.

activity, was once a particularly quiet and secluded country hamlet. Not much remains to remind us of that, apart from those winding roads and their ancient names which are so much a part of the area's heritage. Few parts of Warrington have been so dramatically transformed, but few have such a long history.

LOCAL CHARACTERS

One former Orford resident, Ossie Clark, played a major part in more recent history. Ossie Clark was 'where it was at' in London's 'swinging sixties'. Mick Jagger, Marianne Faithful, Cilla, 'Twiggy' and Lulu were a few of the famous faces who flocked to Quorum, the stylish Chelsea boutique where Clark worked from 1964.

It had been a dramatic arrival onto the scene for future fashion sensation Ossie; born during a German air raid on Walton Hospital, Liverpool. His

71

John Blackburne was lord of the manor of Warrington from 1764 but his real passion lay in botany. At the age of 80 he 'was bright enough to take visitors around the garden and quote Latin and English names of all the plants'. His left hand is proudly pointing to the glasshouse which enabled him to cultivate exotic plants, whilst an earlier pineapple has been painted over.

parents, Ann and Samuel Clark, named their first son Raymond and wisely decided to evacuate the new baby and his three older sisters, Gladys, Kay and Beryl, to the relative safety of Oswaldtwistle, Lancashire. Here the family endured wartime austerity, with food and clothing rationing, relieved by mother's home dressmaking.

In 1949 7-year-old Raymond, and his family, including Carol and Jimmy Melia, children of older sister Kay who had a singing career in faraway London, moved to 5 Sandy Lane West in Orford, then a rural setting, on the outskirts of Warrington. His new Orford classmates at St Margaret's School christened him 'Ossie' because of his broad Oswaldtwistle accent and the nickname was to stay with him for life.

The post-war Warrington of his childhood seemed a typically drab northern town. Yet the presence of the Yanks from Burtonwood brought a glimpse of transatlantic culture: 'American cars with fins and suicide blondes', as Ossie later recalled. The young choirboy from St Oswald's Winwick came to prefer Elvis Presley and Chuck Berry on the jukebox at the Rendezvous Coffee Bar in Sankey Street.

The 1950s teenager Ossie watched the local Teddy boys 'lounging in pink day-glow socks' at the Rodney Street Boys' Club and plotted his escape. Not

Peter Peacock, Mayor of Warrington between 1913 and 1919, was a contemporary rival of Marks & Spencer. In partnership with his brothers he established a chain of Peacock's Stores, trading from a warehouse in West Street, Orford.

for him the 'proper jobs' awaiting an eleven-plus failure and he found an ally in his art tutor, Roy Thomas, at Beamont Technical School. Saturday morning classes at Warrington School of Art helped him secure a place at Art College in Manchester at the age of 16, the first stage in a career in the glamorous world of fashion, far away from Warrington.

CHAPTER SEVEN

BEWSEY, DALLAM AND WHITECROSS

Much of these areas of Warrington had been part of the demesne of the Boteler family, lords of the manor of Warrington from Norman times until the reign of Queen Elizabeth I. A real understanding of the lifestyles of the gentry in times past is often lost to us, because their houses no longer survive or are altered beyond recognition, or because the documents are not as informative as we might like. But that cannot be said of the Butlers of Bewsey Hall, one of the oldest families and oldest houses in the Warrington area. In the year 1579 a remarkable inventory of the entire contents of the house was produced, followed by a survey of the estate in 1587. The Butlers (or Botelers) gained their initial prosperity by serving as butlers to the earls

A view of Bewsey Hall in the late eighteenth century showing the earlier seventeenth-century wing (left) linked to the Georgian extension (right) which was later demolished. By the early 1900s Bewsey had become known as the Old Hall, after Lord Lilford had built a new mansion nearby.

of Chester, and were lords of Warrington from soon after the Norman Conquest. They became important county gentry and by the middle of the thirteenth century had acquired the large landed estate at Bewsey, which became their main residence. Its name is derived from the Norman French word 'Beau See', which means 'the beautiful place'. Archaeological excavations in the period since 1970 have confirmed that there was a small early medieval manor house here, which was extended and rebuilt on several occasions through to the late sixteenth century.

It was a substantial property by that time, one of the largest residences in south-west Lancashire. The inventory was made for probate purposes on the death of Sir Thomas Butler – the rooms were richly furnished and so was the late Sir Thomas, whose clothes included the following:

1 pair of short velvet hose

1 taffeta doublet without sleeves

1 satin doublet

1 pair of long velvet breeches

1 riding cloak lined with unshorn velvet

1 garded [striped] cloth cloak with sleeves

1 Spanish leather jerkin

1 long gown of silk grogram [silk + mohair mix]

1 velvet cloak lined with buckram

Another long gown of wrought velvet

1 short furred camlet gown [angora wool]

An old blue riding cloak

1 pair of riding boots

1 pair of black Jersey stockings

A satin doublet

A white canvas doublet

A taffeta hat

A black felt hat

3 large velvet caps

2 other caps of a lesser sort
6 shirts

It is a rare and vivid glimpse into the appearance of a Warringtonian more than 430 years ago, and we can imagine Sir Thomas riding in style into the town and around the estate, clad in his velvets and silks and fancy caps . . . or maybe looking rather more muddy and scruffy, in his old blue cloak, after

By the 1900s Bewsey Old Hall had declined to a tenanted farmhouse with an uncertain future. Half-forgotten in its historic woods it was reputedly haunted by the ghost of Lady Isabella and a ghostly white rabbit fruitlessly chased by generations of Boteler hunters! A local historian recorded the legend in the 1840s and perhaps later inspired young Lewis Carroll who was living at Daresbury at the time?

a day's hunting across the flat lands and fields of Burtonwood and Bewsey. The house to which he came home had a substantial farm as well – there were thiry-five sheep, fifteen calves, and fifty-four pigs, no fewer than twenty-three horses, with wonderful names, such as White Dutton, Bald Croft, Dun Davy and Blackbeard. Sir Thomas had plenty of ostentatious wealth. There were silver tureens and spoons, basins and salt-cellars. The kitchens were equipped with a huge variety of cooking utensils: great brass pans, immense iron pans to catch the dripping under meat that was roasting on the spit, dozens of smaller basins and dishes, and sixteen heavy pewter saucers (in which, as their name suggests, spicy sauces were served with meat). The great hall was hung with painted cloths and woollen hangings, and there were at least twenty-two feather beds in the house. In Sir Thomas's own bedchamber there was a picture of Christ and a picture of Queen Elizabeth, for he was a loyal subject and a devout Christian. And beyond the house was a great range of outbuildings, including a cheese room, a dairy and a brewhouse. It was not such a bad life.

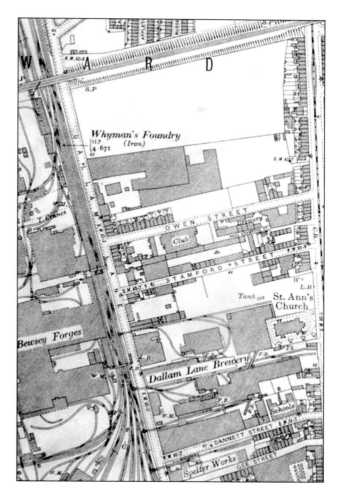

This 1928 Ordnance Survey map shows the concentration of heavy industry near the railway terminal at Dallam.

But of course Bewsey Hall, with its moat and woodlands, extensive grounds and rambling architecture, was only part of the story of this area. Bewsey itself originally came within the large township of Burtonwood, but in the past two hundred years it has been drawn ever closer into the town of Warrington, and is today generally associated with other areas such as Dallam and Whitecross. One important change to the landscape of the area was the construction, in 1757 to 1759, of Britain's first true canal, the Sankey Navigation. The original plan had been to make the Sankey Brook and Dallam Brook navigable to St Helens by building locks on the brook itself, but at a late stage the design was altered to provide for a quite separate channel, fed by the brook but physically distinct. The canal, passing just beyond the wooded surrounds of Bewsey Hall, did not generate new industry and housing in the area, because this part of the district lies just beyond the coalfield which in the years around 1800 was the main catalyst for change,

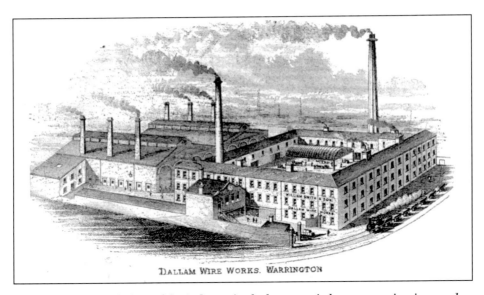

DALLAM WIRE WORKS. WARRINGTON

Until the national decline of the industry in the late twentieth century, wire, iron and steel works were major employers in the Bewsey, Dallam and Whitecross areas – notably Greenings's Britannia Works at Bewsey; Frederick Monks's Whitecross works and subsequently the Lancashire Steel Corporation.

but it remains one of the most important historical monuments in the region. Much more far-reaching in its effects was the construction, seventy years later, of the branch line which linked the Liverpool and Manchester Railway with Dallam, where Warrington's first station was built (the site lies on the north side of Tanners Lane, next to the Dallam Lane junction). Opened in 1831, the little branch line achieved a rapid promotion to glory when, six years later, it became part of the main line to London, and from 1848 was a vital link in the route between Glasgow and the capital. The original branch took a dead-straight line from Winwick Quay south to Tanners Lane, but when the London line was built the alignment was diverted to avoid the built-up area of the town – the pronounced curve just north of Warrington station is the result.

The arrival of the railway opened this area up to commercial and industrial development, and by the 1890s the Dallam area had become a hive of activity. Along Tanners Lane and adjacent streets there were to be found industries of all sorts: tanneries, of course, but also forges and wireworks, rope works and breweries. South of Bewsey Street were the great brickfields which provided the materials from which many of the late Victorian houses of Warrington were built, while the coal yards around the old railway terminus supplied the fuel for those same residential areas. In its concentration of industry, and the variety of trades carried on, Dallam was a key element in Warrington's commercial success.

In the 1830s Bewsey Road was a fashionable residential area of middle-class villas. Industrial development brought neighbourhoods of working-class terraced housing whose occupants were deemed in need of the civilizing influence of religion. This 1960s view at the junction with Froghall Lane shows St Paul's (right, 1831–1984) and Bewsey Road Methodist Chapel (left, 1875–1966).

Meanwhile Whitecross, rather than the fashionable end of the town, had been chosen as the site of the Warrington Union Workhouse, the great institution which was built in 1848–51 to cater for the poor and destitute, including the hundreds of newly arrived Irish migrants fleeing starvation and famine at home. But it was not designed to offer comfort or consolation, for the purpose of the workhouse was to be a fearsome and intimidating deterrent, so unpleasant in its regime and its character that the poor would quickly learn to stand on their own two feet – or that was the optimistic, though severe, perception. The Union Workhouse was at the end of Guardian Street, named not for the local paper but for the Board of Guardians of the Poor of the Warrington Union, the middle-class ratepayers who approved the policies and voted on the expenditure whereby the poor were assisted or turned away.

Built in the late 1840s, in a political climate of severity and harshness, the workhouse had changed by the 1890s, when a more sympathetic official policy allowed a regime which was more humanitarian and understanding. In 1900 the Warrington Union Infirmary was added, consisting of two wards to care for the chronic sick and maternity cases. Later known as Whitecross

These two 1930s scenes prove that Lovely Lane was once lovely indeed!

In 1948 the Borough General hospital was extended at the dawn of the National Health era.

Hospital, the building was taken over by Warrington Borough Council in 1929 and subsequently renamed the Borough General Hospital.

By the mid-twentieth century Warrington Borough Council had also embarked on a major programme to provide improved rented housing on council estates, including the Bewsey and Dallam areas. In July 1927 Warrington's first major estate, 'Bewsey Garden Suburbs', was unveiled. Modelled on the garden city of Letchworth, it was planned with amenities such as schools and recreational facilities for its residents. Further developments followed at Clap Gates Farm and later Dallam in the post-war years. Some new inhabitants felt almost like pioneers until public transport and local shops helped to develop the communities. By the late twentieth century Warrington New Town Development Corporation had developed further housing at Old Hall and almost the last of the former Boteler estates were swallowed up by housing.

In July 1927 the first council houses at Bewsey Garden Suburb stood ready for the official opening by Mayor Arthur Bennett, who had been a leading local advocate for improved working-class housing in a garden setting, away from the crowded courtyards of the town centre.

A view of Dallam's new council housing in the 1950s before television aerials and the private motor car became commonplace.

CHAPTER EIGHT

BANK QUAY
AND SANKEY BRIDGES

For more than three hundred years Bank Quay has been the heart of Warrington's commercial strength. It was here, back in the last decades of the seventeenth century, that new industries began to appear, marking the point at which Warrington began to change from a country market town into one of Britain's first industrial centres. During the next 250 years an extraordinary variety of different trades and industries located along the riverside above and below Bank Quay, and today this zone is still the most heavily industrialized part of Warrington. In the intervening period other industrial districts have come and almost gone, but Bank Quay remains as important now as it has been for centuries.

Explaining why this is so is not difficult, for the river is the key. Since before the Roman period, for thousands of years, the lowest convenient crossing point of the Mersey was at Warrington. Routes converged on the site of what is now Warrington Bridge, where in the distant past there was a relatively shallow ford. But what made it easier for travellers to cross the river made it more difficult for boats, for there was insufficient depth of water to allow any but the smallest vessels higher up the river. This meant that Warrington bridge was the effective head of navigation on the river, and as far as sea-going vessels were concerned the deeper water finished at Bank Quay. That is why the area became so significant, for it was where land and sea met. Shipping, bringing raw materials imported from the rest of the British Isles or from overseas, could dock at the quay itself, while from this point the overland routes fanned out to other parts of northern England, bringing manufactured goods and other materials essential to industrial processing. When, in the eighteenth century, the river was made navigable upstream from Warrington by means of locks and short canal-style cuts, Bank Quay became one of the places where goods could be trans-shipped from sea vessels to river boats.

Given this key role in the regional transport network, it is not surprising that when new industries started to emerge in the reign of William III, Bank Quay was a favoured site. Land transport was relatively slow and expensive, so processing the raw materials beside the river, at the point where they were unloaded, made good sense. We can trace the emergence of the new industrial area from the beginning of the 1690s, when Thomas Patten sponsored

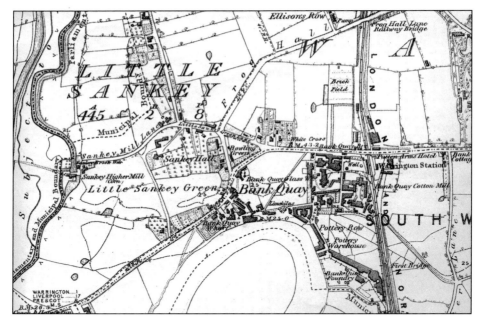

The early industries of Bank Quay and its rural neighbour of Little Sankey are revealed in this 1845 OS map. Clustered around the loop of the River Mersey to the south and the railway line running north–south are the short-lived iron foundry, pottery works and cotton factory together with the soap works, glassworks and flour mill. Nearby lie the open fields, corn mill and old hall of Little Sankey village.

the improvement of the tidal waterway downriver from the quay, and so allowed larger vessels to reach Warrington. Within a few years copper was being smelted there, using ores which came from Alderley Edge, and later from Ecton in Staffordshire and Parys Mountain on Anglesey. Among other uses, the copper was made into wire (boosting an existing local craft towards its status as Warrington's greatest Victorian industry). By the end of the eighteenth century other trades at Bank Quay included glass-making, for which Warrington was briefly more important than St Helens; pottery; and the chemical and soap production which was to be the mainstay of the area in the twentieth century.

As industrial development accelerated, the belt of manufacturing and processing plants gradually extended down the river. If we had visited the area in the late nineteenth century the first plant we would have seen was the Bank Quay cable and rubber works, between the river and the railway at the south end of Bank Quay station, the site later occupied by the Indoor Karting centre. Then there was the chemical works (where Lever Faberge is now) and the flint glass works, the soap works and the cornmill by the waterside. Beyond this, south of Liverpool Road, was the vast and sprawling

Bank Quay in the late 1870s was still relatively underdeveloped. Photographed by William Fell, an early partner in the Crosfield's operations, this view of the wharf shows Fairclough's mill (centre) but little hint of the commercial expansion on the horizon.

Raw materials are being unloaded at Pottery Wharf in the 1870s, although the pottery had already ceased to operate. A colony of Staffordshire potters had been transported to Bank Quay by a pupil of Josiah Wedgwood to take advantage of its excellent transport links. The enterprise had failed by the 1850s and the neighbouring Bank Quay Foundry had taken over the site.

Shipbuilding began at Bank Quay in the 1840s but was equally short-lived. Pictured here is the Tayleur, *built for the White Star Line to carry emigrants to Australia. The largest iron ship then built on the Mersey, she sank on her maiden voyage in 1854, with the loss of 400 lives. The shipyard later became the site of Robinson's glassworks.*

Although Fairclough's mill is still clearly discernible, by the late 1890s Bank Quay wharf was dominated by Crosfield's soap and chemical works. To enable the firm to expand south of the river (left) their transporter bridge is seen here under construction to link the two sites. This flimsy structure was replaced by 1914 by a sturdier version capable of transporting railway wagons, road vehicles, goods and pedestrians.

By 1914 Monks Hall & Co.'s Bank Quay iron and steel works stretched for almost a mile along the Mersey and was served by its own railway sidings. The products of the firm's forge mills, puddling furnaces, welding works, tube works, riveting plant, bedstead and mattress works had a flourishing British and export market. In 1986 the last billet of steel emerged from Number 4 mill and the furnaces were extinguished

complex of the Monks Hall ironworks, with its subsidiaries: the tube works, the rivet works and the bedstead works. In all, this great industrial enterprise stretched for over half a mile along the north bank of the Mersey. Between 1900 and 1930 there was a shortage of space for industrial expansion, and Crosfield's was forced to extend south of the river, taking over the flat on the inside of the great tight bend of the Mersey opposite the old works. The 'island' was linked to the north bank by the remarkable transporter bridge, one of only a handful of such structures in the world.

But Bank Quay was more than just industry, for it was also a community with a highly distinctive identity, one shaped not only by the fact that almost all the menfolk worked in the factories and plants on their very doorsteps, but also by the isolation of the area. When the industries started to develop, in the late seventeenth century, Bank Quay and the riverside were a long way outside Warrington town, which then did not extend beyond Bridge Street and the inner end of Sankey Street. In between lay fields and meadows. By the middle of the eighteenth century a new community was starting to emerge, as little rows of cottages were built immediately alongside the factories and works. Eventually, the industry grew so that it encircled some of these housing areas, which were consequently isolated and overshadowed by works, railway lines and tall chimneys. Cut off from the rest of the area, they were self-contained and had a strong sense of separateness. The most striking example was the group of some fifty-five tiny houses in Glasshouse Row and Factory Lane, tucked away between the glassworks, the soap works and the railway lines south of Bank Quay Bridge. Elsewhere, the terraces and short rows of housing along Liverpool Road in Little Sankey were also in the shadow of the works, linked with Warrington by the tramway but in many senses quite separate from the town.

Sankey Bridges was another industrial community, which had grown up

Many of Bank Quay's workers lived in the shadow of their workplace. Glass House Row, seen here in 1907, was home to employees of Robinson's glassworks.

in the second half of the eighteenth century at the point where the turnpike road to Liverpool crossed not only the Sankey Brook but also, from 1759, the new canal which carried such a heavy coal traffic from St Helens. The canal, the first true canal to be built in Britain during the industrial age, was a major artery, and around the bascule (or lifting) bridge which carried the main road a thriving commercial area developed. As well as the boatyards there was also a complex of limekilns (where lime was burnt, to provide the essential raw material for mortar – every terraced house built in these fast-growing areas required large quantities of that – and also for agricultural use). The Mersey White Lead works, with its massive tall chimney, stood just south of the bridge, and next to that was the Sankey Wireworks. The old core of the community was around the bridge over Sankey Brook but during the mid-Victorian years long terraces of housing were built along Hood Lane and Huntley Street to accommodate the workforce in this miniature industrial centre.

Railway snaked around the district, made present day and night by the puffing of steam engines and the rattle of trucks and wagons. The expresses to and from Scotland roared through Bank Quay, over the high-level bridge that crossed the Mersey and was one of the main landmarks on the journey north, but the heavy freight trains also steamed along the riverside route

The tram route to Sankey Bridges had helped Little Sankey to develop into a suburb of Warrington by the early 1900s. New terraced houses for the workers had swamped the old village, although one half-timbered cottage which had played a significant local role in the English Civil War of the mid-seventeenth century is still visible in the background.

behind the houses on Liverpool Road, and skeins of sidings and mineral lines wove their way through the industrial premises and across the residential streets.

South of the main road the riverside marshes extended downstream from Bank Quay, the now-tidal Mersey flowing in great lazy loops towards the open estuary. The canal at first joined the Sankey Brook just below Sankey Bridges, so that vessels used the whole length of the middle river, but the long meanders, silting channel and shifting sandbanks always presented obstacles to navigation so the St Helens Canal was soon extended along the north shore as far as Fiddlers Ferry, where the river was wider and deeper. The profits were huge, and during the first decades of the nineteenth century the shareholders were receiving dividends of almost 20 per cent per annum. Yet, beyond the belt of industry that stretched from Bank Quay to Sankey Bridges, there were still, a century ago, large areas of open farmland. Sankey Hall, an ancient farmhouse, stood where the great roundabout at the junction of Sankey Way and Lovely Lane is today, and Mill Lane, now a cut-off dead-end, led to the old watermill which stood beside the brook where now it is crossed by Sankey Way.

These older landscapes had survived all the changes of the previous two hundred years, but during the twentieth century further large-scale devel-

The main Liverpool road over the Sankey St Helens Canal was little more than a wide cart track by the early 1900s. The vast chimney of the Mersey White Lead Co. dominates the left of the photograph whilst to the right can be seen the yard of Clare & Ridgway.

The Santa Rosa *is dramatically launched by Clare & Ridgway on 7 July 1906. The Clare family were originally coal merchants and carriers on the canal before opening a boatyard and dry dock at Sankey Bridges. The* Santa Rosa *was one of the last Mersey flats launched at the yard, which continued in business as a repair yard, builders' merchants and timber yard.*

Little Sankey Hall, pictured here in 1917, was a shadow of its former self and engulfed by humble terraced housing. Despite the efforts of conservationists it was demolished in the 1930s and today its site has disappeared under a vast traffic island on the approach to Bank Quay from Liverpool.

Caught in a moment of time by an early twentieth-century photographer, the residents of Green Street are a reminder of the tightly knit Bank Quay community.

From humble beginnings in 1815 the Crosfield family became not only major employers in Warrington but also played a prominent part in Warrington's social and political life. Arthur Crosfield (seen here), the town's former Liberal MP, was knighted in 1915, sold the family firm to former rivals Lever Bros and moved to a magnificent London mansion.

opment, culminating in the creation of the New Town, transformed the district and made it almost unrecognizable. The new dual carriageway has bypassed the older section of Liverpool Road, making it comparatively peaceful after many decades of being a key traffic artery, but the community, now a mixture of older terraced housing and new residential developments, is still compact and self-contained just as it always was. The little pockets of early industrial streets, crammed between the high walls of the works, have long since gone, and now only old maps, historic photographs and fast-fading memories remind us of the first community of Bank Quay. Three centuries and more since the Pattens first began to develop the area, the products of local enterprise (albeit now owned by one of the world's great multinationals) are still being sent from Bank Quay to all the corners of the globe.

CHAPTER NINE

SANKEY AND PENKETH

Further down the river are Great Sankey and Penketh, now one of the largest residential areas in the borough. Historically, these were country districts, far way from the bustle of Warrington town and in a rather remote position on the north side of the estuary. Their inhabitants worked on the land, and even in the late nineteenth century this was primarily an agricultural district, its flat lands dotted with ancient farmhouses and its landscape shaped by the patterns of farming over many centuries. This was an area of mixed farming, with stock-rearing and dairying as well as arable. As Liverpool grew from the mid-seventeenth century onwards, emerging as one of the world's great cities, some farms in this part of the region began to specialize in supplying the urban market with butter and cheese, so that a sizeable trade in dairy produce had developed by 1800. It is perhaps strange to think of south-west Lancashire as a major cheese-producing area, but in the eighteenth and early nineteenth centuries the land north from Warrington through Winwick to Culcheth and Leigh, and westwards through Sankey, Penketh and Bold, was famed far and wide for its cheese, which was generally held to be far superior to Cheshire cheese. That trade ended in the 1840s, with the coming of the railways, for they allowed fresh liquid milk to be sent quickly and efficiently to supply the markets of Liverpool and Manchester. Cheese-making died out and instead, every morning, carts trundled along the lanes of Sankey and Penketh, Bold and Burtonwood, taking churns of milk to the nearest railway stations to be sent down to the goods yards at Edge Hill, Garston and Waterloo.

There was also a great deal of arable farming by the early Victorian period, again encouraged by the expansion of Liverpool. This was one of the few parts of Lancashire and Cheshire where cereal crops were extensively grown – mainly wheat but with some oats and a good deal of barley to supply the great breweries of Warrington. During the nineteenth century a particular local specialism emerged: the raising of potatoes, for which the heavy loamy soil is especially suited and which were sent in large quantities to Liverpool, St Helens and Warrington. Although the major increase in arable farming was a result of urban growth in the region, there was a long tradition of market gardening.

Many of the older farmhouses of the area are no more, having been pulled down during the past hundred years as housing and urban development steadily expanded across their fields and pastures. One site which does

In January 1911 a group of Penketh residents revived the age-old custom of walking (or beating) the parish boundaries to ensure that neighbouring Bold, Great Sankey and Cuerdley had not encroached into Penketh. Starting near Heath Road, the intrepid group crossed brook, canal and river by boat and used their poles to jump ditches and hedges. The occasion ended with a substantial meal at Fiddlers Ferry Inn.

survive in part is Barrow Old Hall, first recorded in 1313 and now remaining as a fine moat in the angle between Billington Close and Barrow Hall Lane, next to the Great Sankey High School. In a 1466 survey of the manor and estates in the Warrington area belonging to Sir Peter Legh the property is described as 'in olden time called Barowhouse', when it had had, among other delights, two barns, a large apple orchard and a garden. In 1859 it was said to be 'an ancient moated mansion, containing many excellent Rooms . . . surrounded by agreeable and productive Gardens and Grounds, with Stables and Outbuildings attached', but sadly it fell into disrepair and was demolished in the early 1920s. However, the moat survived and in 1986–7 was cleaned and restored, with archaeological excavations taking place at the same time to try to establish more of its history. It was shown that the timbered late-medieval hall, which was for centuries one of the possessions of the Bold family of Bold Hall, had been built on sandstone footings and had had a clay floor.

Until the seventeenth century a considerable part of Sankey and Penketh

By the early twentieth century Barrow Old Hall had declined to a picturesque half-ruined farmhouse. The original defensive moat surrounding it had resident ducks and was evidently popular with anglers.

was covered with unenclosed heathland; open rough ground clothed with heather, gorse and coarse grasses. Some parts were very damp and peaty, with patches of undrained mossland and wetland. From the reign of Elizabeth I onwards local landowners and farmers steadily enclosed these wastes, as they were called, carving new fields out of the rough ground, hedging and fencing and draining, and then improving the land to create new pasture and arable. This process carried on well into the nineteenth century, gradually nibbling away at the heaths and commons until finally, in 1869, the remaining hundred acres in Penketh, at Greystone Common and Doe Green, was enclosed and divided up. Today, Doe Green is still on the very edge of the urban area, where the town meets the countryside, but the site of the other common has long since disappeared and now it is recalled only by two road names: Greystone Heath Drive in Great Sankey and Greystone Road in Penketh.

As the enclosure of the heaths progressed, local cottagers and 'ordinary folk' could no longer graze their animals freely on the commons, as they and their ancestors had done for many generations. Being independent-minded and spirited, they were not content to take this passively. During the years before the Civil War of the 1640s there were frequent outbreaks of rioting and popular unrest in these communities, as local people took retaliatory

A relic of medieval Penketh? This ancient windmill was captured by early amateur photographer Thomas Davies in 1855 before it tumbled into decay. Situated at the junction of Stocks Lane and Meeting Lane, it had actually been relocated to Penketh from Gateacre and was still in use as late as 1841 by Thomas Edwardson.

action. In 1629, for example, Thomas Ireland of Bewsey, the lord of the manor, had instructed his men to make new fields on part of Greystone Heath. In mid-March it was discovered that two men from Great Sankey, Thomas Rothwell and Richard Farrer, had been pulling down the hedges and filling in the ditches which the workmen had made, so wrecking the newly enclosed fields. When challenged, they had denounced Ireland and his actions and defiantly proclaimed that they would not let him stand in their way. Such opposition to the local lord could not succeed, for he was too powerful and 'progress' demanded that the heaths should steadily disappear, but it is clear that many local people did not see these changes as being to the good. They stood to lose and they preferred the old and time-honoured ways of doing things.

But for most people life was never settled or comfortable anyway, and just over twenty years after the opposition to the loss of the common land, the two townships were ravaged by a visitation of plague, one of the

Brookside Farm was one of Penketh's many arable farms. By the 1900s it had its own newfangled steam threshing machine, but harvest time was still a labour-intensive affair.

Clock Farm near Cuerdley Cross recorded in the early twentieth century.

One of the earliest photographs of Penketh shows its brewery at about 1870. The 1841 census records that it was operated by the Ardern brothers before being taken over in the 1850s by Mather & Co. It had ceased trading by 1880, bought by Robert Garnett, a devout teetotaller, and was later converted to a tannery.

Penketh Tannery had opened with a workforce of ten in the 1880s who produced 100 hides a week. By 1939 it was a major Penketh employer with 250 hands.

By 1903 Penketh Tannery had become a flourishing concern under the management of Charles E Parker, Garnett's son-in-law. In 1925 the premises were rebuilt and extended after a major fire, emerging as one of the largest single-site tanneries in the country and producing 6,000 hides a week by 1939. Post-war decline in the tanning industry led to its eventual closure in 1958.

A view from Penketh Tannery tower showing the workers' neat terraced houses

greatest curses of the seventeenth century. Coming as it did at the end of a long and bloody Civil War, in which many local people were involved and during a siege of which the town of Warrington was badly damaged, this must have seemed like God's punishment for the wickedness of the world. The people of Great Sankey addressed a petition to the county magistrates in 1652, asking for assistance in their plight (which was partly financial) and saying that

> it pleaseth god to visit Two families in the said town with the Contagious Disease of the Plague which said houses by order from Mr Ireland and Mr Bold have been shut up ever since And one of the families being a poor tradesman a tailor, who lived by his trade and deprived of his liberty, the town hath been forced to maintain him and his family, being five in number, for most part which hath put the Town to extraordinary cost and altogether undone the poor man; and the rest of the poor inhabitants seeing that they have been deprived of going to market at Warrington or else where

Sankey St Mary's Chapel was originally consecrated in 1769 and later remodelled and enlarged. By the early 1900s its surroundings were still rural, continuing the view of local historian William Beamont in 1882 that it was enclosed 'on three sides with a wall of clipped green lime trees, so fitting and so natural as an ornament of a country churchyard'.

The Friends Meeting House in Meeting Lane Penketh, pictured here in the early twentieth century.

Before the state assumed responsibility for education in the early 1900s many local children attended Penketh's Wesleyan Methodist Day School in Chapel Road. Provided by local benefactors, the Garnett family, the elementary school was extended by 1887 to teach 280 children whose curriculum included daily Bible readings. In 1908 it reverted to a Sunday school with the opening of Stocks Lane Council School.

Penketh Co-operative Store, pictured here in 1905, was conveniently situated for its customers at the junction of Farnworth Road, Stocks Lane, Warrington Road and Station Road.

The tranquillity and isolation of Fiddlers Ferry was captured in the early 1860s by Thomas Davies.

Penketh has the distinction of having a character mentioned by Shakespeare (in Richard III). Thomas Penketh was one of the most respected scholars of his day. Honours at Oxford led to a professorship at Padua University in 1474. Returning in triumph to England in 1480 he was made provincial head of the Austin Friars. His sermon in support of usurper Richard III at Easter 1484 led to his downfall.

The magistrates agreed that some financial assistance should be given to compensate the community for the losses which it had incurred. Life was uncertain and hazardous in the past, and though a rural location might seem to be more peaceful and even idyllic, nowhere was exempt from the terror of the plague. One answer was to worship the Lord with fervour and commitment, and this was certainly a God-fearing place. In 1650, two years before the outbreak of plague, a survey undertaken by commissioners appointed by Parliament reported that the inhabitants of Great Sankey and Penketh had jointly, at their own expense, recently built a new chapel. Odd though it may now seem, the two townships were at this time part of the vast and unwieldy parish of Prescot, and their nearest place of worship had been Farnworth. During the 1640s and 1650s, when the Nonconformists were in power, the chapel was used for Presbyterian and Puritan worship and after the Restoration, when the Church of England was again dominant, it was probably disused for long periods. In 1728 it was officially taken over by the Anglicans and in 1765–9 rebuilt and dedicated to St Mary. Yet this relatively remote and secluded area continued to be a stronghold of dissent. In 1667 and 1669 George Fox, the founding father of the Society of Friends or Quakers, visited Sankey and Penketh and started a Quaker meeting, and in 1681 a meeting-house was built in a very secluded place, far out in the middle

Robert Garnett (1805–77), pictured here with his family, was one of Penketh's major benefactors. A devout Methodist, he made his wealth from property and his cabinet-making business. His prestigious showrooms were in Sankey Street (later occupied by Woolworths) but his workshops were sited in Penketh where they employed many villagers. He was so well regarded that over 600 mourners attended his funeral.

of the fields on the corner of what are now Meeting Lane and Greystone Road.

And beyond even the farming hamlets of Sankey and Penketh was Cuerdley, where the flat expanses of the riverside marshes, often flooded, always wet, were edged by the great river with its broad sands, shifting shoals and lonely creeks, bringing the waters of half the Pennines to the sea. For many generations this was one of the most hauntingly remote places in north-west England, known only to fishermen and wildfowlers, the small number of local people and those who carefully navigated the boats up and down river. But in the late eighteenth century industrialization began to make its mark. The canal cut through the marshes down to Fiddlers Ferry, where since ancient times a small boat had carried travellers across the wide river. In the 1830s the town of Widnes began to grow rapidly and made its presence felt, as the fumes from its huge chemical works were carried upriver on the wind. The railway came in the 1850s, breaking the silence of the marshes, and in the 1890s the Manchester Ship Canal was cut along the opposite shore, so ocean-going vessels now added variety to the view. But the really great change took place in the early 1960s with the construction of the immense power station on the north shore, with its twin clusters of four cooling towers each, and its plethora of pylons and electricity grid lines. One of the most prominent landmarks in the region, visible from vantage points many miles away and dominating the lowlands of the riverside, this is the largest building in the whole of Warrington borough.

CHAPTER TEN

WILDERSPOOL, STOCKTON HEATH AND WALTON

Wilderspool was ancient before Warrington even existed. Although changes in the past two and a half centuries have made it difficult to visualize what the landscape must have looked like two thousand years ago, it is clear that in the prehistoric and early Roman periods the river valley was wide and flat-bottomed, with extensive marshes and wetlands making

Thomas May unearths Wilderspool's Roman past in the early 1900s. Without the sophisticated resources available to the archaeologists of Time Team, *May managed to reveal sizeable areas of industrial settlement at Stockton Heath and Wilderspool. Much valuable evidence of Roman settlement was undoubtedly destroyed by the excavation of the Manchester Ship Canal and May's theory of the existence of a Roman fort at Wilderspool remains unproven.*

By the late 1780s Wilderspool was the focus for new industry with the arrival of Greenall's brewery on the earlier Roman site. This aerial view of 1901 shows the distinctive clock tower which formed part of the 1880s rebuilding and expansion. On the horizon new terraced housing is appearing in Stockton Heath village whilst London Road itself is eerily free of traffic.

it difficult to cross. But at Wilderspool, where the river flowed in a great double bend, a tongue of slightly higher ground extended northwards more or less along the line of what is now the Causeway, and allowed closer access to the river. At the foot of today's Bridge Street a band of solid sandstone came down to the water's edge, where there was a relatively convenient fording place. These two factors meant that an early routeway developed across the marshes, and this focused north–south traffic on the axis of Bridge Street and the Causeway. Although there was another ford at Howley, one which for several centuries was of equal importance, the direct alignment along the Causeway eventually dominated – and it is no coincidence that it was that route which was followed by those supreme engineers and builders, the Romans, when they constructed the great road that headed north from Middlewich, across mid-Cheshire, over the river and then into Lancashire.

Wilderspool was the first major industrial centre in the history of north-west England. Almost two thousand years ago it emerged as an important Roman settlement, a town with a large riverside manufacturing and ware-housing zone, with potteries, iron-working, lead-working and masonry

Greenall's dray horse would soon give way to a fleet of Sentinel steam lorries to serve the brewery's expanding chain of public houses.

An idyllic rural scene at Lumb Brook Bridge, captured in the early twentieth century by local artist Oswald Garside as an inspiration for a potential water colour painting.

workshops. It is remarkably similar, in the work it did and the site it occupied, to the industrial belt that grew up from the end of the seventeenth century on the opposite bank of the river, and extensive archaeological excavations have confirmed that there were other similarities. People lived cheek by jowl with housing, the town was unplanned and congested, and there were problems of pollution, waste disposal and overcrowding. The Romans chose the spot for precisely the same reasons as their distant descendants, 1500 years later – it stood at the head of navigation for seagoing vessels, at the place where the main road crossed the river, so it had ready access to imported materials and a good distribution network for finished goods and manufactures. Pottery from Wilderspool has been found as far afield as Hadrian's Wall, while pigs of lead from Flintshire, which were destined for Wilderspool but lost overboard or in a shipwreck, have on occasion been found in the riverbed above Runcorn. But by about AD 350 Wilderspool was, like Roman control itself, in rapid decline, and five hundred years later, when trade and commerce again picked up, the preferred location for settlement and business was on the north bank where the great town of Warrington started to grow.

Long before heavy goods lorries rumbled along London Road, the Bridgewater Canal had made London Bridge the focus of an earlier regional transport network. Horse-drawn barges carried passengers and goods between Stockton Heath quayside and Manchester. By the time of this early 1930s photograph goods traffic was already declining and passengers had long since found swifter methods of transport.

*This tranquil scene of the early 1900s is barely recognizable as Victoria Square!
Renamed in honour of Queen Victoria's Diamond Jubilee of 1897 the area had
previously been known to locals as Pigeon Bank. The horse bus was soon replaced by
trams which necessitated the demolition of Beaconsfield Terrace (left). The Old
Mulberry Tree Inn (centre) was rebuilt in 1907.*

*The excavation of the Manchester Ship Canal in the early 1890s had a dramatic effect
on the landscape of Wilderspool and Stockton Heath. The 'Big Ditch' and its swing
bridges left industrial Wilderspool in Lancashire and marooned Stockton Heath in
rural Cheshire. This dramatic photograph captures the sheer scale of the operation,
with the white-shirted 'navvies' toiling like ants on the giant spoil heaps.*

Not until the early eighteenth century did Wilderspool re-emerge as a developing industrial and residential area, serving as the southern extension of Warrington 'across the water'. There were two focal points in the growing community. One was a group of cottages at the junction of the London and Chester roads, a site later largely obliterated by the construction of the ship canal – it was roughly where Stafford Road and Greenalls Avenue meet the southern end of the Causeway. The other settlement was on the edge of Stockton Heath, at what is now Victoria Square. The whole of this area then lay in the township of Appleton, while Wilderspool proper was part of Latchford township, which extended as far as the southern end of Warrington Bridge. The boundary between the two was the little Lumb Brook, flowing down the slopes behind Dale Lane to Chester Road, and then sluggishly across the valley floor to join the river close to where Loushers Lane meets the Causeway. Much of this area was transformed from the 1760s as new transport links brought new industry. The turning point, perhaps, was the building of the Bridgewater Canal along the slopes on the southern side of the valley in 1765–75. This created a new focal point for growth, at London Bridge, while the improvements to the river and, in 1803, the opening of the Runcorn and Latchford Canal which cut across the valley bottom from the later site of Kingsway Bridge, under Knutsford road at Black Bear Bridge,

London Road was realigned with the cutting of the Manchester Ship Canal, completed in 1894. Soon the old road over Twenty Steps Bridge on the Runcorn and Latchford Canal (left) would disappear to be replaced by the new straighter route over the swing bridge (right).

This aerial view from Wilderspool Brewery tower shows Stockton Heath in about 1900. Over the Ship Canal new bay-fronted villas are appearing to house the new professionals and white-collar workers eager to escape from the heart of industrial Warrington to a leafy suburb.

and then through Wilderspool, brought new growth. In 1786 the main road to Chester was turnpiked and in 1820 what was to become the modern A49 heading south to Stretton and mid-Cheshire. This increased the amount of traffic funnelled down to the bridge at Warrington. Wilderspool and the adjacent area became a transport hub, a meeting place of land and water routes.

Stockton Heath had no official identity as yet. On Peter Burdett's map of Cheshire, published in 1772, it is not even named, although he does mark Broom Field, Hill Cliff and Belfield, each names which have continued in use to the present day. The heath itself had gone by the 1770s, but had spread across the slopes of the hill at the western end of Stockton Lane, and the tiny settlement which gave its name to the place was the scattered agricultural community between Lumb Brook and Sandy Lane. The result of these changes was a gradual increase in the number of houses, and in particular in the vicinity of London Bridge and the road junction which is now Victoria Square. Stockton Heath began to emerge as a distinct community. In its early days it was noted for its craft industries. Attached to many of the cottages in the area were workshops in which filemakers and toolmakers undertook their highly skilled and specialized trades. The district was an important outpost of the Warrington file and tool industry, a world leader

By 1902 Warrington's tram network had reached Stafford Road on the Wilderspool side of the canal, leaving Stockton Heath's residents to trudge over the swing bridge. Here in 1904 workmen are laying the new track which would allow commuters to board the tram in Victoria Square until the arrival of motor buses in 1931.

Whitefield Road at the junction with Walton Road was typical of the superior housing appearing on the outskirts of Stockton Heath by the First World War.

By the census of 1841 Gilbert Greenall was in residence at Walton Hall, pictured here in Twycross's Mansions of the County Palatine of Chester. By 1870 a Scottish baronial-style wing was added to the Elizabethan first phase to accommodate the children of his second marriage and the enlarged household necessary to serve a Member of Parliament and a baronet.

The Bridgewater Canal linked Stockton Heath to neighbouring Walton but both were also part of Greenall territory. The brewing family had their headquarters in Wilderspool, were patrons of St Thomas' Church and school but had their family seat at Walton.

from the 1780s onwards, and even in the late nineteenth century the trade still survived in the district. From at least 1749, too, there had been a brewery at the place where the Causeway turned into London Road, and in the early 1780s this was taken over by a consortium led by Thomas Greenall. In 1791 the premises were completely rebuilt on a grand scale and within a few years the brewery had become one the largest employers in the town, a position it retained until the 1960s.

The most dramatic alteration in the character and appearance of Stockton Heath came in 1885, when work began on the construction of the Manchester Ship Canal. This massive project, the greatest civil engineering work in late nineteenth-century Britain, was completed in 1894. The canal chopped through Stockton Heath and Grappenhall with a massive broad cutting (much larger than it appears today, because of the depth of the water). It required the diversion of the old Chester road, huge swing bridges on the new Chester Road and London Road, and the alterations to other canals and the Mersey meant that the great loop of the river alongside the causeway was abandoned and truncated. The ship canal severed Wilderspool from

The era of the 'horseless carriage' had arrived in Stockton Heath in 1909. Perhaps these curious residents would have been less eager to see the vehicle if they could have foreseen the impact the motor car was to have on the village by the end of the century?

This view across the lake shows Walton Hall about 1900, at the time of the marriage of Sir Gilbert Greenall's heir (also called Gilbert) to Frances Griffiths. Sir Gilbert and Lady Frances turned Walton into a model estate, with prize-winning herds of Kerry cattle, Large White pigs and extensive stabling. Lady Frances established botanical gardens at Walton which later became pleasure gardens for generations of Warringtonians.

Stockton Heath and became one of the dominant barriers to communications in the district, the notorious swing bridge being the cause of major traffic jams even when the motor age was in its infancy.

By this time Stockton Heath was starting to emerge as a favoured residential area. Although it had the older core of small housing and a narrow grid pattern of streets immediately south of Ellesmere Road and Fairfield Road, the development in the Edwardian period began to assume a 'quality' tone and local estate agents increasingly considered that Stockton Heath, like Grappenhall, was an address which could be marketed.

By 1914 there was new housing of 'superior' quality in areas such as Walton Road and Ackers Road, and the first signs of suburban residential development were creeping outwards along London Road, up the hill away from the crossroads and London Bridge. Many of the houses built in this period, and through the 1920s and 1930s, were aimed at the lower middle-class market – white-collar workers from Warrington's industries who wanted to live outside the noisy and congested central areas, away from terraced housing that opened straight onto the street. This period, from the

Sir Gilbert Greenall (1806–94) had assumed a controlling interest in the family brewery in 1848, a year after he was first elected Conservative MP for Warrington. He served in Parliament and local government for over thirty years, being rewarded with a baronetcy in 1876. He was also a devout Anglican and a benefactor of many local churches, including St John's Walton which he built and endowed in 1885.

1880s to the 1920s, marked the beginning of the trend towards moving to the Cheshire side of the valley. During the 1930s and, after the interruption of the Second World War, the 1950s, this trend accelerated and the upper parts of Stockton Heath, towards Appleton, became one of the most favoured residential areas in the district. By 1960 many large detached and some semi-detached properties formed a ribbon of development along London Road as far south as Stretton village, and new suburbs had grown up in Hillcliffe, Cobbs and the Lyons Lane area, taking advantage of the elevated position with wooded surroundings and attractive views.

Over to the west was Walton, which until the late nineteenth century was divided into two townships stretching down the slope from Hatton to the river and owned by the Brookes of Norton. Lower Walton, or Walton Inferior, was itself split in half when the Manchester Ship Canal was built, and the northern part was transferred to Warrington. The southern part, now joined with Higher Walton (or, more grandly, Walton Superior), remained as a rural parish within Cheshire until the reorganization of local

Sir Gilbert Greenall, Lord Daresbury (1867–1938), followed in his father's footsteps, but took a less overt political role. His preferred lifestyle was that of a country gentleman, agriculturalist, leading figure in equestrian circles and stock breeder. His characteristic style of dress was 'almost exactly the popular conception of a farmer squire'. King George V conferred a peerage on him in 1927 and he took the title Baron Daresbury of Walton.

government in 1974, when it too was brought within the boundaries of Warrington borough. Lower Walton, once a small country hamlet at a crossroads near the river, became part of the built-up area and merged into Stockton Heath.

Higher Walton was dominated by the Walton Hall estate, which stretched from the old Warrington Road to Houghs Lane. The medieval estate had been landscaped in the eighteenth century to create a large park with long grassy slopes and carefully placed copses and woodland belts to enhance the view and screen the estate, while from the 1770s the Bridgewater Canal contoured along the hillside at the lower end. Edward Greenall purchased Walton in 1814 (together with part of Daresbury and Higher Whitley). By 1840 a new Greenall country seat had been built. This mansion was described by a contemporary as 'a handsome structure of Elizabethan architecture in

Frances, Lady Daresbury, was a formidable figure. An accomplished horsewoman and keenly interested in agriculture, she also brought boundless energy and organizational flair to a wide range of local associations. More abrasive and outspoken than her genial husband, she was a true-blue Conservative, widely respected by her political opponents. Her death in 1953 'severed the last link in the chain binding this industrial town with traditional English Country life'.

brick, with stone facings upon the angles and gables'. Its dramatic spiky profile, with pinnacles, turrets and elaborate balustrades, gave it a grand and imposing air which in the early twentieth century was matched by the dramatic profile and no less imposing air of its formidable chatelaine, Lady Greenall.

CHAPTER ELEVEN

APPLETON, STRETTON AND HATTON

Along the ridge south of the river there were three ancient townships – Appleton, Stretton and Hatton – which only became part of Warrington borough in 1974. Before then, for over a thousand years, they had been part of Cheshire. The three have shared a common history, as agricultural communities which in the late twentieth century were increasingly subject to outside pressures and where development gradually began to alter the older landscapes. Nevertheless, these remain some of the most rural parts of the present borough and there are plenty of traces of the past still to be found. Although they are increasingly orientated towards Warrington, the three villages are linked by an ancient routeway which runs east to west along the ridge and is now marked by Cartridge Lane, Grappenhall Lane, Stretton Road and Hatton Lane. There is a network of other byways and lanes across the area, some of them now altered by the demands of modern traffic but others, such as Green Lane at Appleton Thorn and Goose Lane at Hatton, retaining much of their ancient character.

Behind the ridge were large tracts of poorly drained mossland on the plateau top, and a few small patches of scrub and rough vegetation still survive in this area – most notably at Appleton Moss and Stretton Moss, just south of the M56, where names such as Moss Hall and Mosswood Hall also remind us of the past landscape. Other names tell their own stories. Stretton, for example, means 'the settlement on the street' – but this refers to the old Roman road which ran south from Wilderspool towards Middlewich and then down into the West Midlands. This great trunk route of the Roman period can still be traced as the long straight alignment of London Road, from Quarry Lane to the Owens Corner roundabout, then by the footpath that runs direct to Stretton church and on to Spark Hall, at which point it is interrupted by the motorway and the associated road diversions.

Some of the old landscape disappeared with the construction of the wartime airfield at Appleton, and a good deal more when the M6 and M56 were built and the young offenders' institution and trading estates were developed between the motorway and Grappenhall Lane. In the late 1960s the boundaries of Warrington New Town were drawn to include much of the undeveloped countryside between the built-up area and the motorway, and this part of the area was designated for major new housing projects with an

Burdett's map of Cheshire in 1772 shows a network of rural lanes, often no more than farm tracks, which linked the small hamlets to the south of Warrington. The motor car has made this seem an integrated landscape but in 1772 each settlement had its distinct identity.

emphasis on the private sector. As a result, networks of attractively land-scaped and sinuous new roads have been built across the slopes, taking advantage of the varied topography, and communities such as Pewterspear and Dudlow's Green emerged after 1975. Until the late 1950s the grounds of Appleton Hall occupied much of the land south of Lyons Lane. When the new housing projects were developed in this area, and across the farmland to the east towards Grappenhall, stretches of woodland and the narrow steep-sided valleys or dingles (the north Cheshire dialect word) which dissect the slopes were retained, most importantly along the Dobb's Brook and Dingle Brook, so that there is plenty of open space and a commendably varied and interesting design has been achieved.

A countrywoman draws water from Appleton Well in the mid-1850s. Appleton, Hill Cliffe and High Warren have since become major reservoirs for Warrington.

The village of Appleton Cross developed at an age-old crossroads, possibly dating back to Roman times. In 1365 Adam de Dutton erected a marker cross there but by this early twentieth-century photograph only the stones which had originally supported a wooden cross remained.

Appleton Hall (seen here in the early 1900s) had been built by Thomas Lyon of the wealthy Lyon family in 1820. Lyon was a successful businessman with an interest in Greenall's brewery and Parr's bank but adopted the role of the squire of a country estate. Appleton Hall remained central to village life until the sale of the estate in 1944 and demolition of the mansion in the 1950s.

A picturesque view of Stretton Hall c.1900, typical of Cheshire's black and white half-timbered farmhouses. Rebuilt in the reign of Elizabeth I it had been home to the Starkey family who owned the manor of Stretton until the early eighteenth century. A sale catalogue of 1884 described it as 'an excellent country residence for a gentleman however good his position'.

All aboard the Stretton to Whitley motor bus as the era of the horseless carriage arrived to link these outlying villages.

In 1880 Robert Bateman was commissioned by Roland-Egerton Warburton of Arley Hall to paint this romantic picture of the revival of the ancient ceremony of Bawming the Thorn on the occasion of Roland's marriage. Adam de Dutton, who was an ancestor of the Warburton family, had become lord of the manor of Appleton over six centuries earlier and links between the Arley estate and Appleton remained until the 1960s.

Archdeacon Richard Greenall was the twin brother of Gilbert, MP for Warrington, and had become rector of Stretton in 1831. In 1855 he married Elizabeth Lyon of Appleton Hall, uniting two prominent wealthy local families. He commissioned prominent architect Gilbert Scott to begin rebuilding the chancel of St Matthew's in 1859 and on Richard's death in 1867 the rest of the church was rebuilt as his memorial.

Bawming the Thorn is a unique annual ceremony at the village of Appleton Thorn. On or near to St Peter's Day on 29 June local children decorate or 'bawm' a special thorn tree with red ribbons and garlands of fresh flowers. The ceremony began when Adam de Dutton, the medieval lord of the manor, planted a sprig of the Glastonbury Thorn (said to have been sprung from Christ's Crown of Thorns).

Beyond, the older agricultural landscapes survive, with a series of old farms, especially around Hatton. There, the name Bluecoat Farm recalls the old Warrington Bluecoat School, which was endowed with this land on its foundation in the early 1670s. The school received the rents from the farmland and this money went towards the upkeep of the building (next to Holy Trinity Church in Sankey Street) and the master's salary. The landscape of small rectangular fields was largely a creation of the sixteenth and seventeenth centuries, when this was developing as an area of profitable pastoral farming, part of the great Cheshire dairying belt. Substantial areas survive, and these are now among the most precious landscapes within the borough of Warrington, a reminder of quiet rural worlds which over most of the district have long since disappeared.

CHAPTER TWELVE

LYMM AND DISTRICT

Towards the eastern end of the present borough of Warrington is the small town of Lymm, a place with a long and fascinating history. The church of St Mary, dramatically perched on an outcrop of sandstone high above Lymm Dam, is one of the most ancient religious sites in north Cheshire. The Bradley Brook here carved its way through a narrow gorge with high rocky sides, a landscape unlike anything else in the region. This outstanding natural feature, with its cliffs, caves and rushing torrent, may have had a special importance in the early Christian era and perhaps even before then, so the ritual significance of the location of the church is probably thousands of years old. The greater part of the gorge has now been flooded so that the full visual impact has been lost, but its remarkable qualities are still very apparent. We know that in the early Christian period many much older sacred sites were 'adopted' by the new faith, providing continuities with the old ways and making conversion much easier and less painful, and Lymm is probably a fine example of this process.

This early Victorian engraving of Lymm by W Hawthornwaite shows the new dam below St Mary's Church.

Lymm Hall, seen here in the late nineteenth century, was originally the manorial home of the de Limme family but was rebuilt in the times of Elizabeth I by the Domville family.

Lymm Dam is now a much-cherished and extremely popular amenity, a lovely landscape even though it is man-made. In 1821 the road from Warrington to Altrincham and Stockport was made into a turnpike in order to improve the route between these fast-growing urban centres. At Lymm the old road wound awkwardly down the steep hill of Eagle Brow and then up again along Pepper Lane or Rectory Lane. For heavy industrial traffic this was a difficult route, so the turnpike trustees built a new stretch of road – a pioneering bypass – cutting out the bends and hills and spanning the valley below the church with an embankment and new bridge. This gave the opportunity to create a very large new reservoir, the dam, which could provide water supplies to Lymm's industries. In 1824 the work was completed, the gorge was partly flooded, and the surrounding slopes were soon landscaped, for they were part of the Lymm Hall estate. In 1848 the land south of the church was sold to George Dewhurst, a very wealthy Manchester cotton merchant, and he built a fine new mansion, Beechwood (where the rugby ground is today). The work of 1821–4 therefore provided three major benefits: a fast new road, an industrial water supply and a beautiful new landscape. It transformed Lymm and was an important factor in the town's growth as a favoured residential area.

The Bridgewater Canal was a new trade artery running through the parish of Lymm from the mid-eighteenth century until pleasure craft took over two centuries later.

But Lymm was also an industrial centre of some importance. Below the main road the brook flows through the rocky steep-sided Dingle, along which is the Lower (or Bottom) Dam, the original millpond which supplied the town's large water-powered cornmill. At the centre of the village, below the cornmill, it became known as Slitten Brook, the name referring to the slitting mills which stood below the aqueduct. These were where iron bars and sheets were cut by water-powered saws to form strips of metal, used for nailmaking, or the narrow bands of iron with which barrels were bound. There was once a third great millpond within the gorge, which was a popular local beauty spot in the Victorian period, but in the early twentieth century its dam collapsed and it was drained. Lymm was also a centre of fustian-cutting, a highly skilled and intricate process which was one of the finishing trades in the textile industry. Fustian (a mixed fibre cloth usually of cotton and linen) was woven with a high pile made up of minute loops of thread. In cutting it, a very long, very narrow and immensely sharp knife blade was run through the countless thousands of loops, slitting every one of them and producing a cloth with a soft surface: velvet, velveteen and corduroy are popular names for such cloth. In Lymm and the nearby villages until the early twentieth century this craft was practised by women who walked up and down the long tables on which the cloth was spread, slicing through the loops and using only their extraordinary judgement with the naked eye to train and guide the passage of the knife.

Other changes came to Lymm in the eighteenth century. In 1759 work began on the construction of the Bridgewater Canal, which was intended to link Manchester with the lower Mersey and bypass, or compete with, the Mersey and Irwell Navigation which had been opened twenty years earlier. The canal meandered its way across the countryside of north Cheshire, contouring at 90 feet above sea level along the gentle slopes on the southern side of the Mersey valley and skilfully engineered to avoid the need for locks – there are none between Worsley and Runcorn, and this is one of the longest lock-free stretches of any English waterway. The choice of the contour route meant that the canal headed for the middle of Lymm, crossing the brook on a substantial aqueduct and severing the parish in two. While at the time this probably seemed disruptive (imagine the outcry if it were to be proposed today!) in retrospect it was a further advantage to the town. Now it forms a particularly attractive stretch of waterway, part of the very popular Cheshire Ring route, and with its towpath a favourite walk. The canal brought trade to Lymm – a wharf was built immediately east of the aqueduct

This early photograph of Lymm in 1860 records a village in transition. The focal point is Lymm's ancient cross, with the sandstone steps worn down by centuries of footsteps. To its left are the ancient village stocks where generations of wrongdoers had been humiliated and punished. In the background new shops for an expanding population dwarf their older neighbour to the right.

By 1900 yet more shops huddled around Lymm Cross, which had been restored to commemorate Queen Victoria's Diamond Jubilee of 1897. Distinguished architects Paley & Austin had been commissioned to reface the worn steps, replace the acorn-shaped finials and substitute a symbolic golden crown on the weather vane in place of the old cockerel.

and there was a modest amount of canalside warehousing – but fortunately it did not lead to the creation of a new industrial area and today few would argue that its construction was anything but a benefit to the town.

At the centre of the village is its ancient cross, which dates from (depending on which version you accept) the fourteenth or the seventeenth century, and is set on steps carved from the red sandstone on which the town is built. The cross and stocks stand at the main road junction. Lymm was never officially a market town, but it is very likely that in the Middle Ages and into the eighteenth century the wide space around the cross at the foot of Pepper Lane was an informal trading place, where country people came to sell their wares – eggs, cheese, vegetables and fowls – and where the social life of the community was centred. Lymm was a notably attractive place, with its combination of beautiful natural scenery, historic buildings and a quaint medieval street pattern. It was partly for this reason that in the early nineteenth century it began to emerge as a favourite residential area for wealthy merchants, businessmen and professionals from the Manchester area and Warrington. Unlike Altrincham and Wilmslow it did not have a particularly fast or frequent rail service, and the railway came only in 1853, which was relatively late, so it never developed as a large dormitory town.

This meant that only the elite could really afford to live here, and in the later Victorian period areas such as Brookfield Road and Booth Hall Lane were developed with very large detached houses set in extensive grounds, a classic piece of expensive Cheshire townscape.

Lymm was also lucky in that the Manchester Ship Canal, that greatest of all local engineering triumphs, passed some distance to the north. Slicing across the flatter lands of the middle Mersey, the canal produced massive disruption. The old course of the river took a great southward loop from opposite Rixton Old Hall, where the River Bollin flowed into the Mersey, and it passed close to Statham and within half a mile of Lymm. This long detour had already been short-circuited in the late eighteenth century by the building of a short cut across the neck of the bend. When the ship canal was constructed a century later the old loop was completely abandoned and silted up, its course now visible only in the short creek off the canal at the north-west corner of the golf course at Statham, and a few nearby short stretches of overgrown muddy ditch. Indeed, until the county boundary was altered to follow the line of the ship canal, rather than the old river, most of the golf course was actually in Lancashire. Statham itself was a small country hamlet in the early eighteenth century, but it grew a little with the coming of the Bridgewater Canal, and a little more with the arrival of the railway.

A similar pattern can be seen at Oughtrington, which was once a scatter of farms and cottages but by the late Victorian period had a saltworks, a railway station and a thick sprinkling of semi-detached villas, detached

The rushbearing ceremony in the 1840s shows Lymm's rush cart drawn by the traditional grey horses.

A large crowd turned out at Lymm Cross in the early 1900s to watch the morris dancers taking part in the rushbearing procession.

houses and short terraces along the roads leading to the railway. The landscape of this part of the district has always had a rather unplanned, random quality, an air of being not quite countryside and not quite town, something which the ever-heavier traffic along the A6144 does nothing to dispel. It was once a quiet country lane, but the development of the huge industrial plants and estates at Carrington and Partington over the boundary in Trafford, and the motorway junction to the south of Lymm, means that it now carries an endless stream of vehicles for which its alignment and width are hardly suited. The railway has now gone, finally closing in the late 1980s though passenger services were withdrawn as long ago as 1962. Today the track of the railway has been converted into the Transpennine Trail and long-distance cycleway, part of the route which enters Warrington borough at Fiddlers Ferry and mainly follows the canal towpaths and disused railway routes through to Broadheath.

Lymm in the early twenty-first century has a population approaching 10,000 and has grown considerably in the past thirty years with the development of new housing areas between Rushgreen Road and the canal, around Longbutts Lane, and on the edges of Statham, Oughtrington and Booth's Hill. Even so, its location away from commuter railway lines and the easiest main roads into Manchester helped to protect it from the full impact of residential growth in the late twentieth century. Furthermore, it was not part of the designated area of the late 1960s Warrington New Town and so was

The cobbled village streets of Lymm at the turn of the twentieth century, before the motor car disturbed its tranquillity. The fine half-timbered building on the right later became the Spread Eagle Hotel.

Lymm Station seems distinctly over-manned in this early twentieth-century view. The branch line never became a busy commuter route but was typical of many of Cheshire's rural lines which fell victim to the closures of the 1960s.

This idyllic rural scene shows the old school house at Statham at the turn of the twentieth century.

never selected for large-scale expansion of the sort which has so much changed areas such as Stockton Heath and Appleton. Lymm retains not only a strong visual identity and distinctive character, but also a powerful sense of history and tradition.

Local customs

Rushbearing is an ancient ceremony held at Lymm each August at the feast of St Mary. Traditionally the church floor would be covered in rushes to help keep the parishioners feet warm during the cold winter months. Ormerod, writing in 1813–19, gave a vivid contemporary account of the ceremony as it took place in an earlier and more rural Lymm.

> This ceremony consists of carrying the church rushes intended to be strewed on the clay floor under the benches, which are piled neatly up in a cart, and a person constantly attends to pare the edges with a hay knife if disordered in progress. The cart and the horse, which are carefully selected from various village teams, are decorated with flowers and ribands. On the rushes sit persons holding garlands, intended to ornament the church for the ensuing year. These are composed of hoops slung round a pole, connected with cross strings, which are concealed by artificial flowers, paper and tinsel . . . The cart so loaded, goes round to the neighbouring hamlets preceded by male and female

Morris Dancers, who perform a peculiar dance at each house, and are attended by a man in female attire . . . who jingles a bell to a tune, and holds out a large wooden ladle for money. As night approaches the cart, with its attendants, returns to the town where the church is situated, and the garlands are fixed, whilst a peal is rung on the bells, and a concourse of village revellers is attracted to view the spectacle.

CHAPTER THIRTEEN

THELWALL AND GRAPPENHALL

Eleven centuries ago this was a war zone. North of the Mersey was a no man's land, a frontier district which had once lain on the southern edge of the great Anglo-Saxon kingdom of Northumbria, whose kings ruled from far-distant Bamburgh on the coast near Berwick-on-Tweed. Now, at the beginning of the tenth century, Northumbria had been overrun by the Norsemen, the Vikings who ruled from York. To the south of the river was a land which, nominally at least, was part of a different kingdom, Mercia, with its capital at Tamworth and its cathedral city at Lichfield. But Mercia had been attacked by the Danes from the east and was now facing the Scandinavians to the north as well. Its Cheshire territories were some of the last major areas under English control. The Mercians were ruled by the redoubtable Aethelflead, a daughter of Alfred the Great, and between 905 and 920 she and her brother, the English king Edward the Elder (reigned 899–925) oversaw the construction of a series of fortified frontier outposts, known as burhs, to act as the frontline against attack from the north. From Chester in the west to Bakewell in the east, the northern boundary of Mercia was defended. One of the forts was at Runcorn, another at Manchester.

In between, guarding a vital strategic crossing place on the Mersey, was a burh at Thelwall, built in 919. Its exact location is now uncertain, though

Thelwall's village pub reflects the history of its village. The Pickering Arms recalls the family which became the major landowners in 1662 but an inscription on the gable end of the half-timbered building recalls an earlier history: 'In the year 923 King Edward the Elder founded a city here and called it Thelwall.'

137

historians and archaeologists have speculated and investigated the question for over two hundred years. The likelihood is that the shifting course of the river has eroded the site and washed away the traces. Current opinion is that the most likely location was somewhere close to Thelwall Eyes, the great flat marshy former island which lies immediately across the Ship Canal from the centre of the modern village. There an old routeway (its course marked by the alignment of Cinder Lane, Halfacre Lane and Bell Lane) came down to the river on firm ground, and then headed, by a way across the marshes, to Woolston. Thelwall was a special place. It had an ancient chapel, but the little township and chapelry were part of the territory of the parish of Runcorn, another crucial crossing point. Historians now accept that this arrangement ensured that the two places, so important to national security, were firmly under the control of the lords of Halton, while Warrington, the other major crossing place, was a royal possession and therefore also secure.

Much remains to be discovered about this fascinating and tantalizing period in the history of the area, but there is no doubt at all that the river crossing made Thelwall a place of very great significance. That 1048 years later work began, half a mile upriver, on the construction of one of the most famous landmarks of twentieth-century Britain is a particularly neat historical turn of fate. Thelwall Viaduct is a key point in the road network

Thelwall residents stroll in the sunshine, passing the post office and shop which were at the heart of village life.

for precisely the same reasons that the fortified burh, its site almost at the feet of the great bridge, was hastily thrown up long before the Norman Conquest. Crossing the Mersey was a challenge and the motorway builders of the late 1950s met the challenge triumphantly. The magnificence of the bridge is hardly appreciated by the tens of thousands who everyday drive across it, and can only be seen from below or, best of all perhaps, from the deck of a vessel on the Ship Canal above which it soars 93 feet. It was hardly the fault of those who designed the viaduct that by the late 1980s traffic on the road had grown to such levels that a second parallel viaduct was required, immediately upstream from the original. The meeting of motorways from six directions, together with crucial local traffic, has made Thelwall perhaps the single most important nodal point on the national road system, though the building of the second bridge has substantially reduced the frequency of standstill congestion.

Below the viaduct the course of the river has been changed many times, not least by the construction of the artificial cuts across the meanders during the eighteenth century and the Ship Canal in the 1890s. The watery landscape of marshes, floodlands and channels was once regarded merely as a dumping ground for waste and industrial debris, but more recently its major importance as wildlife habitat, and the necessity for its protection and

All Saints Church was rebuilt in 1843 in the fashionable gothic style, thanks to the generosity of William Nicholson of Thelwall Hall. By the 1890s a chancel had been added and subsequently stained-glass windows were dedicated as memorials to other prominent local families, notably Warrington wire manufacturers the Rylands family.

COUNTRY
LODGINGS,
TO BE
LET
IN THELWALL,

By the Week, Month, or Year;

PARTICULARS TO BE HAD AT MERSEY MILLS.

The Village of Thelwall is noted for good Water, a salubrious Air, and the Longevity of its Inhabitants.

HADDOCKS, PRINTERS, WARRINGTON.

A Victorian poster proclaims the benefits of living in Thelwall but during the construction of the Manchester Ship Canal in the early 1890s a basic hospital was constructed there for the navvies suffering from an outbreak of smallpox which ravaged nearby Warrington.

Thelwall Hall (seen here in the 1930s) was a fine Georgian-style hall, built by the Pickering family. Sadly it fell into decay after military occupation in the Second World War and was eventually demolished in the 1950s.

Known locally as 'Oyster Hall', Cuerden Hall was home to the Naylor family who had made their wealth as timber merchants.

It is not unusual to see traffic at a halt on Thelwall Viaduct but pedestrians normally walk there at their peril! Motorway travel was still a novelty at the opening ceremony in 1963 so the hard shoulder became a giant car park while families wandered over to inspect this engineering triumph.

enhancement, has been better appreciated. The Eyes, the great tracts of marsh, scrub and open water which lie between the old river and the canal, are relatively inaccessible and cannot be used for building or development because they are so wet, so they are ideally suited to nature conservation. As the river becomes cleaner this role will develop further – the fact that the occasional salmon now swims up the Mersey is a small but heartening sign of real progress.

Grappenhall is known to too many people only as an elongated traffic queue on the main road into Warrington from the motorway, its landmarks provided especially by the swing bridge on Knutsford Road and the monumental high girder bridge which carries the old railway line over the canal (and they are really Latchford anyway). Old Grappenhall is tucked away off the main road and few people who rush down the A50 are even aware of its existence. The church of St Wilfrid is another very ancient foundation, its dedication telling us that it probably dates from the eighth or ninth centuries (for Wilfrid, who in the mid-660s at the synod of Whitby placed the English Church under the control and government of Rome, was one of the leading saints of the later Anglo-Saxon period). Like Thelwall, Grappenhall parish, which included Latchford, probably originally belonged to Runcorn, but it had become separate and independent by the thirteenth century. There are other signs of great antiquity: in the Grappenhall area some of Cheshire's most significant prehistoric sites have been identified, including several Bronze Age burial cairns and barrows, with numerous

Grappenhall was one of the earliest areas settled in the Warrington area and in the 1930s these Bronze Age cremation urns and quern stone for grinding grain were recovered from a burial mound off Euclid Avenue.

In 1859 pioneering local photographer Thomas Davies recorded the heart of Grappenhall village, with its cobbled street and parish church. Although much modified over the centuries, St Wilfrid's Church still reflected the village's medieval history with ancient stained glass and an effigy of a Norman knight. A stone cat carved on the church tower may have inspired Lewis Carroll's Cheshire Cat as his father, the Revd Dodgson, often visited the church.

The 1840s rural splendour of Grappenhall Hall is illustrated here in Twycross's Mansions of the County.

bronze artefacts. These may be associated with settlement on the southern edge of the Mersey marshes (which once extended across the valley floor around Westy and Victoria Park) close to the crossing point which gave Latchford ('the ford by the boggy stream') its name. The name Grappenhall probably means 'the flat damp ground by the river, with ditches', and presumably refers to the same watery lands along the edge of the Mersey.

The old village was centred on the church and the winding stretch of Church Lane, but as with other communities in the area its setting was transformed in the early 1760s when the Bridgewater Canal was dug along the contour, skirting the church and the old cottages and, we can see in retrospect, providing protection from development. Even now it is striking how the suburban housing of the twentieth century stops at the canal. The canal did bring some industry, for Grappenhall Tannery was opened in the early nineteenth century on the north bank (where Brackenwood Mews and Hazelwood Mews are today), with the larger Cliff Lane Tanneries at the Knutsford Road canal bridge. However, Grappenhall was too far from central Warrington and from the river to experience heavy industrialization and that too helped to keep its atmosphere relatively unaltered.

CHAPTER FOURTEEN

PADGATE, FEARNHEAD, WOOLSTON AND NEIGHBOURHOOD

In 1907 the editor of the *Victoria County History of Lancashire* was very rude about Padgate and the surrounding district. He said that this was 'uninteresting country, flat and devoid of trees. There is nothing picturesque enough to induce the passer-by to revisit the neighbourhood.' That seems to have been a view held by other writers, for there are few early descriptions of the area, and it lay somewhat off the beaten track, although the main road to Manchester was of course a busy thoroughfare. The name Padgate is from

It is hard to believe that this undeveloped scene is now the busy junction of King Edward Street and Padgate Lane, but the familiar King and Queen pub in the background provides the clue. On 1 November 1909 Mrs Burrell had a double celebration, for not only was she able to vote for the first time in the local elections but she also went for a spin in a newfangled horseless carriage and her son Walter was on had to record the occasion.

two Old English words, meaning 'path' and 'way or road', and it refers to the ancient route which led north-eastwards from Warrington via Fearnhead towards Culcheth, Leigh and, ultimately, Bolton. This was 'the pad-gate', or Padgate Lane, and it gave its name to the place. Administratively the area was within the ancient township of Poulton with Fearnhead: the name Poulton is now almost forgotten, but it was the area which extended from the river at Kingsway North, through Paddington and Bruche, to Padgate station and Birchwood Way. Fearnhead means 'the higher land covered with ferns', the area referred to being the low hill around Cinnamon Brow which, many centuries ago, more obviously stood above the surrounding damp lowlands.

In the sixteenth and seventeenth centuries the Padgate area lay beyond the end of the town of Warrington (the houses only reached as far as the junction of Church Street and Manchester Road) and was purely agricultural. It had been a wild tract of heathland and common, interspersed with patches of moss and pockets of improved farmland, but even in 1600 this was one of the most desolate parts of the Warrington district. Then the pressures for agricultural change began to make their mark. Landowners, aware of the profits to be made from creating new farmland, and renting it out, contemplated the enclosure of the commons. As they gradually made fields out of the open heath, and planted hedges, dug drains and founded farms, a new landscape emerged. Why is Fearnhead Lane, between Padgate High School and Nook Lane, so straight? The answer is that in the years around 1620 the old trackway across the common was realigned as the land around was enclosed. This caused major local controversy, and in 1627 it was alleged that

> the Common or waste groundes called Fernhead Common lyinge in Fernhead is latelie inclosed and the kinges higheway over the same leadinge betwixt Warington & Culcheth thereby much straitened [narrowed] By reason whereof the same waies are become verie fowle & almost impassable.

Until that time local people had wandered freely across the commons and the track was wide and irregular. When the lane was laid out on its new straight but narrower route the traffic was funnelled along it but, because nobody was willing to pay for its upkeep, it had become a quagmire of mud and potholes and filth. The solution arrived at was that all the people who owned or tenanted the new farmland alongside the road should pay for its repair. They refused to do so, and for many years afterwards there was stalemate. Only in the early eighteenth century did the township authorities agree to maintain the road at public expense.

The landscape of the area survived relatively unaltered even into the middle years of the nineteenth century, but it was changed for ever by

146

Padgate Station in the early 1900s had very few local residents to serve and the late twentieth-century Harpers Lane estate is still a distant prospect.

In the early 1920s communities all around Warrington had a sombre new local landmark in their midst. Here Padgate residents pay their respects to neighbours lost during the First World War at the new war memorial on land donated by the Bennett family. In the background are the new shops and old Stocks Inn which form part of the new settlement near Padgate Station.

Fearnhead Lane may have been a major thoroughfare but it was still relatively traffic-free in 1905. Meanwhile a lone carthorse waits patiently outside the Farmer's Arms for his driver to appear.

In April 1939 over 300 acres of Padgate farmland were converted to a training camp for RAF recruits. In the first fortnight of the war alone, 3,040 men completed eight weeks basic training under the command of Group Captain Insall. By 1943 1,500 recruits passed through the camp each week. The camp finally closed in 1957, leaving acres of derelict land which would be redeveloped as school, shopping precinct and homes in the 1980s.

Warrington New Town Development Corporation begins work on the Long Barn area in 1974.

Bruche Hall and estate off Manchester Road had come down in the world by the twentieth century. Originally the home of the Bruche family, then the powerful Leghs, it passed from the ownership of the gentry to local businessmen before being sold to the Roman Catholic Church. The hall was demolished in the 1960s and today only Bruche Park remains.

Reward poster issued in 1791 for the capture of those guilty of highway robbery and murder at Woolston.

When a large grey seal was seen swimming at Paddington Lock in June 1908 there was great excitement. Sadly, attitude to wildlife in danger was less enlightened then than now. It was trapped, shot, stuffed and presented to Warrington Museum where it is now a local celebrity!

Between Bruche and Woolston lay the more recent district of Paddington, created by a nineteenth-century soap manufacturer. Despite the pleasant open countryside around Paddington Lock, Paddington was chiefly known for the noxious smells coming from Gorton's Bone Works, seen here in 1970.

the construction of the Cheshire Lines Railway. This was promoted jointly by three railway companies – the Great Northern, the Manchester Sheffield and Lincolnshire, and the Midland – which were the arch-rivals and bitter enemies of the London and North Western Railway which owned the old main line from Liverpool to Manchester (opened in 1830). The three companies collaborated, or conspired, to break the LNWR monopoly over traffic between the two cities, and in 1873 opened the Cheshire Lines route, which slashed straight as an arrow across the flat lands of the Mersey valley. So important to their plan was the inter-city traffic (for freight and passengers) that it was originally intended not to serve Warrington directly and to be content with a station at Longford Street. Local protests meant that the loop line through Warrington Central was built instead, with a direct line from Padgate to Bewsey following in 1883. Around Padgate station a small community of villas and cottages began to grow, straggling along Padgate Lane and Station Road.

At the centre of the Poulton half of the township was Bruche Hall, which is first recorded as early as 1219. The estate was owned from at least 1300 by the Bruche family, who became leading figures in the Warrington area as

Between Padgate and Woolston lay a green lane where in 1880 the Warrington Board of Guardians opened Padgate Cottage Homes and Industrial School to accommodate orphans and other children under their care. Boys and girls, even in family groups, were segregated and housed in groups of fifty children. Some found their time in residence traumatic but others felt well cared for. In 1954 the institution was closed as new patterns of childcare emerged.

prominent landowners. They were closely related by marriage to the Leghs, who in the fifteenth century were among the most important families in Cheshire and south Lancashire, and they enjoyed a very troubled relationship with the Botelers of Bewsey, who were local rivals. Unfortunately the Bruches of Bruche came to a bad end. In the 1580s Roger Bruche was notorious as a gambler, who was addicted to dicing, gaming and betting on cockfights. He owed £200 by 1590, a huge sum (maybe £250,000 in modern terms). His kinsman, Peter Legh, paid off the debts on condition that Bruche never again played dice or cards, or gambled for amounts of more than a shilling (5p). Eventually, Legh acquired the estate itself and the Bruches were left almost penniless!

Beside the Woolston New Cut half a mile away a soap works had been opened in 1820 by Jonathan Jackson, a Warrington sailcloth manufacturer. Soap was one of the great new growth industries of the early nineteenth century and all sorts of local entrepreneurs were trying to cash in on this. Jackson's partner, Robert Halton, called the site Paddington, because of his west London connections, and although the soap works went bankrupt after only four years (mainly because Jackson and Halton were operating a tax fiddle which was exposed by the government excise office) the name of the

Attached to Padgate Cottage Homes was an Industrial School where the boys were taught a trade of tailoring or shoemaking. Others worked on the land whilst girls were taught washing, cookery and housework. All residents received a good general education but the chief philosophy was to ensure that they could leave equipped for employment and not become a burden on the state.

area stuck. The soap works became a chemical factory but the name Soapery Row survived for the row of tiny terraced houses, immediately west of Spittle Bridge on what is now the bypassed portion of Manchester road, which is where the workers lived.

LOCAL CHARACTERS

The stories of two people associated with Bruche reveal the worst and the best of human life; the first is the tale of a young postboy, murdered in the eighteenth century and the second the story of a twentieth-century accountant and politician who tried to make his town a better place for all.

The tale of the Woolston highwayman may have echoes of the legendary Dick Turpin but in real life highwaymen were nothing more than common criminals with scant regard for human life. In the early hours of Thursday 15 September 1791 a young postboy rode out of Warrington carrying mail (and money) bound for Manchester. Along the Woolston Road he was set upon by two men, beaten about the head, stabbed and pulled from his horse,

Further down Green Lane lay scattered farms, including Holes Lane Farm, which would later give its name to a housing estate as Warrington's urban sprawl continued.

and left lying face down in a brook with his hands tied behind him. The victim, James Hogwarth, subsequently died from his injuries (or possibly drowned). Warrington was shocked by the incident, not least because he left behind a pregnant young widow. The Post Office offered a substantial reward of £200 for the capture of his assailants, although their concern was more to prevent further robberies. Subsequently suspicion fell upon Edward Miles and his associates, although the evidence connecting them to the murder might nowadays be regarded as circumstantial. Miles and Thomas Fleming were eventually brought to trial at Lancaster Assizes and sentenced to hang for the crime. The judge ordered that an example should be made of Miles, the ringleader. His body was taken back to the scene of the crime and encased in a metal skeleton suspended from a wooden gibbet post to warn future attackers of postboys of the fate which would await them. In reality Hogwarth's colleagues were probably more scared by the experience of riding down Manchester Road on a dark and stormy night and hearing the gibbet irons creaking in the wind.

An altogether more heart-warming character was Arthur Bennett of Bruche and Paddington, who rose to prominence in public life but used his authority for the benefit of others, as his obituary revealed:

> If every public man of Warrington had done as much for his town as had Alderman Bennett, Warrington would be a better place than it is

An affectionate caricature of Arthur Bennett who lived at Paddington House and campaigned to improve Warrington and the lives of Warringtonians.

today. And if a man can live 69 years in the town of his birth and can go hence leaving not one enemy behind he is a man for the loss of whom we are poorer.

Bennett was born in Padgate in 1862 and retained a long association with his birthplace and especially Padgate Methodist Chapel. His father was a wealthy cattle dealer at Bruche but Arthur's career lay in accountancy; although he probably spent as much time on his unofficial career as a journalist. He wrote for the *Warrington Examiner*, the *Sunrise Press* and edited the *Dawn*, producing articles in poetry and prose on his views about Warrington's decline from the country town he had known as a boy to an industrial town where the poor lived in insanitary housing. He mourned the passing of the historic townscape: 'it was a pain for him to see the most

Rural Woolston in the early twentieth century as workers at Holes Lane Farm take a well-earned break to pose for the camera.

insignificant relic of old Warrington discarded'. He was an independent Conservative, being elected to the local council in 1893 and becoming subsequently an alderman and twice mayor between 1925 and 1927. He served tirelessly on countless committees, promoted the building of Warrington Bridge, the redevelopment of Market Gate and the building of good-quality council housing, and campaigned for the corporation to buy public parks at Orford, St Elphin's and Bruche. He was also keenly interested in art and architecture, supported Warrington's Museum and Library and rubbed shoulders with major figures in national literary and artistic circles.

No matter what event there was of importance in Warrington the slight figure with the slight limp; the face with the slightly wistful expression; the thin hand with the almost inevitable cigarette, were to be seen there.

CHAPTER FIFTEEN

WINWICK, CULCHETH AND CROFT

O ne way of passing the time if you're stuck in a long traffic queue on Winwick Road might be to think about all the people who have travelled that way before you. Changes to the road itself make it less obvious than it used to be that Winwick Road heads straight out of the town centre northwards. That is because it follows the line of a Roman road, itself probably on the alignment of a prehistoric trackway. Almost two thousand years ago soldiers marched along Winwick Road, making for the next Roman settlement, Wigan, and perhaps beyond that – the road led eventually to the northern frontier of the Empire itself, at Hadrian's Wall. Coming in the opposite direction we might well have seen trundling lumbering coal-carts,

Winwick and its neighbourhood was one of the earliest areas of human settlement around Warrington. This burial mound at Southworth Hall, excavated in 1980, revealed cremations dating back to about 1500 BC, whilst bronze axeheads, a dagger blade and ring were recovered from sites at Winwick, Culcheth and Kenyon Hall in the nineteenth century.

for we know that the Romans mined coal in the Wigan area and burned it as a fuel in the industrial hearths of Wilderspool. During the next nineteen centuries the road saw armies marching to and fro: Edward I in the 1290s, leading his English forces against the Scots; his son, Edward II, coming with a great retinue in 1322 to deal with lawlessness and unrest in mid-Lancashire; Parliamentarians fighting the king's troops for control of Warrington in 1643 and 1644; a raggle-taggle of fleeing Royalists trying to escape Oliver Cromwell's vengeance after defeat at the Battle of Preston in 1648 – and in between times untold numbers of ordinary people passing along on foot, on horseback, in carts and carriages. By 1800 the road saw more than sixty stagecoaches every day, rattling along with horns sounding and painted varnished bodywork gleaming. It would be farfetched to claim romance for Winwick Road today – frustration is a more likely emotion – but this road has a remarkable and vividly colourful history.

Heading north, the first great landmark that every traveller encountered, from the eighth century onwards, was Winwick Church (though today the motorway junction has intruded its all too visible presence on the journey). The oldest part of the parish church of St Oswald, Winwick, now dates from the fourteenth century, and much of the building was 'restored' or re-constructed at various times in the Victorian period, but its impressive and imposing presence and the richness and splendour of its decoration all speak of a very large and important medieval church. Its history goes back almost to the earliest period of Christian worship in north-west England, and there

In 1905 Winwick Church was regarded as 'Lane Ends' for weary local travellers who could pause to refresh themselves at the drinking fountain erected in memory of John Thompson, an earlier surveyor of the highways.

This picturesque thatched cottage was typical of many which still survived in rural Winwick at the turn of the twentieth century. The two 'dames' seen near the doorway provided basic education for the youngest local children before more formal state education was introduced.

was probably a church of some sort here by 700. The dedication to St Oswald reminds us of this, for this saint was the great king of Northumbria who in 642 was killed in battle against the combined forces of the Mercians and their Welsh allies at a place called Maserfelth, almost certainly the modern Makerfield and so just north of Winwick itself.

Centuries later Winwick church was celebrated for its tremendous wealth: the living was said to be the richest in the kingdom, and in the mid-seventeenth century the rector had an income of over £660, or well over £100,000 a year in modern terms. This meant that some very important people were connected with the church: in the mid-1520s the rector was Thomas Winter, the illegitimate son of Cardinal Wolsey, and on many occasions between 1400 and 1855 members of the Stanley family (the earls of Derby) were rectors – indeed, continuously from 1740 to 1855. Because of its great wealth and extreme antiquity, and perhaps because it was such a prominent local landmark, many legends gathered around Winwick church. One of those concerned the origin of the name. It was said that when the first church was being built, on a different site, a pig was seen running around and shrieking Wee-ick, Wee-ick. It picked up a stone and ran with it to another place, dropping it on the spot where the body of Oswald had been found. The builders saw this as a miraculous sign, and built their church in that place instead. In fact, the name Winwick was not given to us by a pig, but means 'the dairy farm belonging to Wineca', which is more accurate but a lot less entertaining.

The Winwick Broad Oak was a national landmark until its destruction in a gale on 4 February 1850. It is said that 1,000 soldiers once sheltered under its branches, which spread 99 feet from north to south. In 1811 a public dinner was held beneath it to commemorate the heroic actions of local celebrity Admiral Sir Phipps Hornby in capturing a French vessel during the Napoleonic War.

The scale of the 'new' Winwick rectory reflected the status of Winwick Church and the influence of its wealthy patrons, the Hornby family. By 1902 the park in which it stood had become the site of the new county asylum.

Winwick is now a major road junction, but this is a recent development, dating only from the early 1960s and the building of the motorway link road. The ancient focus of the community was Winwick Green, just north of the church along Green Lane between the Newton and Golborne roads. The green has now gone, but its shape can be traced in the way that the houses and cottages north and south of the lane stand well back from the road – they used to be on the edge of the green, their front gardens marking its former extent. This seemingly innocuous place has a dark past. On 19 August 1648, Oliver Cromwell and his army pursued the defeated Scots and Royalist forces down the main road from Preston. The Scots, led by the Duke of Hamilton, made a last stand against the Parliamentary forces at Red Bank, a narrow stretch of lane halfway between Newton and Winwick. They held out against Cromwell for several hours but were eventually forced southwards. According to a contemporary account, Cromwell's forces 'drove them up to that little green place of ground just short of Winwick church and there they made a great slaughter of them'. Cromwell himself reported that about a thousand of the enemy had been killed there and at Red Bank, and that about two thousand prisoners were taken, many being incarcerated temporarily in the church itself.

Winwick, like other places in the rural areas around Warrington, survived almost unchanged from the seventeenth to the late nineteenth centuries. The only major alteration came in 1868, when the new Warrington Waterworks was opened just north-east of the village. It used deep wells to tap the aquifer in the sandstone bedrock, with a pumping station to send the fresh clean water supplies down by gravity to thirsty Warrington. However, towards the end of the century Lancashire County Council was searching for a new location in which to build a great asylum. It was particularly anxious to find a site in south–central Lancashire, and in 1894 negotiated a deal with the Hornby family, owners of Winwick Hall and patrons of the living, to buy a substantial estate including the hall itself and much of the land on the west side of Newton Road, a total of 207 acres. Between 1895 and 1902 the county asylum was built there, the old hall being demolished and the beautiful parkland developed as a self-contained community with a carefully designed layout to accord with the prevailing ideas about the care of the mentally ill and mentally disabled. The asylum, like others in the county, was huge – in 1915 it had over 2,100 patients and by 1950, with some 3,000 residents and staff, it was as large as a small town. By the end of the twentieth century the philosophy of mental health care had changed: large institutions were no longer acceptable, and in 1999 the hospital closed. Its grounds were ripe for residential development and now a new and exclusive housing area has been added to Winwick and its landscape.

East of Winwick there was once a land of small hamlets and lonely farmhouses, of cottages scattered along narrow winding back lanes. This was an almost unknown and forgotten corner of Lancashire, a place which few people from outside ever visited. There was a whole series of little communities here: Croft and Southworth, Middleton and Arbury, Houghton and Peasfurlong. As late as 1905 the population of the whole of that area was little more than 1,500, and the lanes in Middleton and Houghton were described as merely 'cart tracks'. The area was flat, open and with few woods or trees, though many long stretches of hawthorn hedges. It produced potatoes, wheat and oats, with some market gardening. The remoteness and seclusion of the area had for many generations made it a fertile ground for those who did not follow the establishment line in matters of religion. After the Reformation, for example, Southworth Hall was a noted stronghold of Catholicism and during the later sixteenth century and throughout the seventeenth the Southworth family suffered heavy fines and persecution for their faith. The house had a private chapel which was served by Jesuit priests, and in the eighteenth century it not only became one of the most important centres for the revival of Roman Catholicism in Lancashire, but also passed into the ownership (until 1820) of the great Catholic school at Stonyhurst in the Ribble Valley. Elsewhere in the area were Nonconformist congregations which, like those of the Catholic faith, had to keep a low profile and met away from the prying gaze of the authorities.

The peace and tranquillity of these small communities lasted even into years after the Second World War. No railways crossed the area – the nearest to the south was the Cheshire Lines route through Padgate and Orford, to the north the main Liverpool and Manchester line at Kenyon. Hardly a soul outside the immediate area was aware of the existence of this forgotten corner. But up in Preston and down in London there were those who, looking at their maps, began to design the transformation of this world. In 1949 the county council published a volume by James Drake, the county surveyor, entitled *Road Plan for Lancashire*. Building upon pre-war sketches, it argued that Lancashire, and the nation, desperately need a completely new network of what it called 'motorways', and that central to the success of any such strategy was the construction of a new road which would run from mid-Cheshire, over the Mersey at a small village named Thelwall, then through the little-visited, thinly populated backwater of Croft, Houghton and Southworth, to Haydock, Wigan, Preston and the Scottish border, with a new link road to Winwick. The fate of this peaceful area was determined, for the government accepted the plan and the M6 project was born. In 1953 the orders for building the new road were made, and in 1958 the route from Preston to Thelwall was confirmed. Work began in September 1959 and in July 1963 this stretch of the M6 was completed.

By that time survey work on a new motorway from Liverpool to Hull was beginning. The building of the M62 began in September 1971: the section from Liverpool to Croft opened in November 1973, and thence to Worsley in August 1974. Croft interchange, where the two motorways meet, is one of the largest junctions on the British motorway network, having gobbled up hundreds of acres of farmland with its skein of link roads. Peace had gone, never to return. As work on the M6 was completed, and the design of the M62 was in progress, the next great change got under way. Warrington was designated as a new town in 1966, its boundaries drawn widely to allow large-scale housing, industrial and commercial development beyond the edge of the old town. One of the most important areas for expansion was to be the swathe of rural and semi-rural land between Orford and the two motorways, so that over the next thirty years much of the open country in the southern part of the old township of Middleton, Arbury and Houghton was reshaped to emerge as the Cinnamon Brow and Houghton Green residential districts. North of the motorway the older landscape is relatively untouched, but to the south it has almost disappeared – and no matter where you are, the continuous sound of heavy traffic on the M6 means that you cannot be unaware of its nearness.

Further to the north-east is Culcheth, a very ancient community which is first recorded in the early thirteenth century. Its name is far older, for it derives from the Celtic words 'cul-coed', meaning 'narrow wood': this was the language spoken by the British inhabitants of the area before the Anglo-Saxon colonization of the seventh century. Culcheth township was large and

Sundial House dated from the 1690s and had served first as a school before becoming the parish workhouse. It was a prominent landmark in Culcheth village until its demolition in the 1970s to make way for the shopping centre which came to bear its name.

This early twentieth-century photograph of Culcheth Hall shows it at after remodelling by the Withington family who acquired the building in 1824. Parts of the building were much older, dating back to the early thirteenth century when it was occupied by the de Culcheth family who were the local lords of the manor. The building was demolished in the 1950s but an avenue of trees planted by the Withingtons remained.

thinly populated, historically divided into four 'quarters': Culcheth village, Holcroft, Peasfurlong and Risley. It was a small community – even in 1901 fewer than 2,500 people lived in the whole area from the main railway line in the north to Risley Moss in the south – and it had little connection with Warrington or, indeed, with any other place. It was in the parish of Winwick, but was so far from any place of worship that in the late medieval period a small chapel, dedicated to the Holy Trinity, had been built close to Culcheth village to serve the scattered inhabitants of this wide rural area. Newchurch, as it was known, did not become a parish in its own right until 1845, but here, as in the neighbouring townships, there were in any case many devout Catholics after the Reformation, steadfast and unswerving in their faith, and Culcheth was a notable and early stronghold of Methodism, Unitarianism and other Nonconformist denominations. With broad tracts of mossland to the south, the huge and seemingly limitless flatness of the great Chat Moss to the east, and the wet and boggy valley of the Glazebrook to the north, Culcheth was physically isolated like no other community in the Warrington area.

It had a little industry – the mid-Victorian Daisy Bank Cotton Mill was the successor to linen-weaving which had flourished as a domestic trade in the eighteenth century – but it was not really part of the great south Lancashire industrial economy. Even the opening of a railway did little to

Daisy Bank Cotton Mill (earlier known as Clayton's Mill), built in the 1850s, was one of two mills providing employment for Culcheth's inhabitants.

alter the sense of separateness, for the line in question was the Wigan Junction Railway, a misguided attempt by the partners in the Cheshire Lines company to gain access to the lucrative coalfield of mid-Lancashire. In 1879 they opened a freight line which ran from Glazebrook to Wigan. Passengers were so unimportant that no service was provided for them until 1884. With its inconvenient route, and infrequent and slow service the railway did little to attract potential customers, and had almost no impact upon Culcheth. It closed in 1964, but it had enjoyed a short period of glory when, during and immediately after the Second World War, it provided the main access to the huge munitions works at Risley. That story is told in the next section, but it is also part of Culcheth's history, for the Risley factories drew a large number of workers to the district. During the period from 1945 to 1960 Culcheth village grew very rapidly into a small town, as new housing estates were built to accommodate the workforce at Risley. Today the growth continues, although at a slower rate, and Culcheth has become a sizeable, though still very much self-contained, community.

LOCAL CHARACTERS

Culcheth has at least one claim to fame – or infamy – in its association with the notorious Colonel Blood who stole the crown jewels! In 1650 Thomas

165

Blood had married Maria, eldest daughter of Colonel John Holcroft, a major Culcheth landowner and leading local supporter of Parliament in the Civil War against King Charles I. In 1648 Cromwell's Parliamentary troops, including the dashing young Irish Lieutenant Blood, were pursuing the remnants of a Royalist army at Winwick. Blood met Holcroft who later rued the day he invited the young Irishman back to Holcroft Hall where he captivated the eldest daughter Maria. Despite parental disapproval Maria and Blood were married at the parish church of Newchurch on 21 June 1650.

All seemed to go well until Charles II was returned to the throne in 1660 and Blood lost his lands in Ireland and was dismissed from the army. Leaving his wife and two children at Holcroft Blood went off to seek revenge against the king. An unsuccessful attempt to capture Dublin Castle led to flight to Holland, Scotland and eventually London, where he even became a spy for the Duke of Buckingham, one of the king's advisers. By 1670 he was an outlaw with a royal reward offered for his capture after a series of daring escapades. Rather than going into hiding he launched his most audacious plan of all: to breach the security of the Tower of London, seize the crown jewels and hold them to ransom! A first attempt with Maria as a decoy failed so he returned with son Thomas and other accomplices. This time they succeeded in making off with the jewels, but were swiftly caught and Blood was found to have the royal crown under his cloak. Against all the odds Blood escaped the king's wrath, thanks to Buckingham, his powerful ally at court. He was not only pardoned for his crime but had his Irish estates returned with a pension too and became a folk hero.

Chapter Sixteen

Risley, Birchwood and District

On maps of the early twentieth century the area on both sides of the main railway line east of Padgate is almost empty of habitation and settlement. To the south was the expanse of Woolston Moss and Rixton Moss, extending as far as the Manchester road, while to the north Risley Moss reached uninterrupted as far as the Glazebrook. Along the brook there was a narrow belt of farmland with a few scattered houses and two larger properties, Great Woolden Hall and Little Woolden Hall, and then there were the immense levels of Chat Moss, carrying on for another six miles to the edge of the Manchester conurbation. The mosslands were the outstanding feature of the geography and landscape of this part of the county and had been the subject of comment for centuries: back in the reign of Henry VIII the traveller and antiquarian John Leland had written of them in tones of wonder and fear, while in the 1820s Stephenson's proposal to cross the northern part of the mosses with his planned Liverpool and Manchester railway had provoked scorn, derision and – when he succeeded – amazed admiration.

For local people the mosses had been a valuable economic asset because of their seemingly unlimited supplies of peat (which was the main fuel of the district) and because they provided rushes and reeds for thatching, wetland pools and brooks for fishing and wildfowling, and, on the drier fringes, area of rough vegetation for grazing cattle. Since the seventeenth century landowners and those bent on improvement had sought to drain and reclaim the mosses, but the challenges were great and even a hundred years ago substantial areas remained in their virgin state. There were a few patches of damp woodland on Risley Moss and Rixton Moss, but the landscape was a mournful and lonely one, of flat tracts of wet peat and scrub or no less flat and no less peaty fields, edged with long straight hedges and long straight drainage channels. When the Cheshire Lines Railway was built across the area in the 1860s, and the line from Glazebrook through Culcheth in the 1870s, they had to be supported on massive embankments that swallowed up vast quantities of earth, and elaborate networks of dykes were constructed to drain away at least some of the water. By the 1920s some tramways had been built out across the mosses, light and temporary constructions on which horse-drawn wagons could carry away the peat from commercial working for use in horticulture, but otherwise the mosslands remained largely empty.

Then came the rise of Nazi Germany, the threat of war and the desperate need to build up Britain's armed forces and, no less urgent, its armaments industry. By the end of 1938 the War Office and the Royal Ordnance were seeking sites for huge new munitions factories, looking for areas of cheap land which was of little value (since to use farmland would compromise the anticipated need to feed a hungry nation). The sites had to be close to main railway routes, but away from centres of population, partly for security reasons but also for safety. The mosses at Risley were selected as one such site, and in the spring of 1939 work began on a huge new industrial complex, stretching almost two miles by one mile and served by a special branch line from Newchurch Halt near Culcheth, on the railway from Glazebrook, and a private station at Birchwood on the main Liverpool–Warrington Central–Manchester line. The complex opened in January 1940, and within two years was employing over 4,000 people. There were few people on the spot – that, after all, was one of the reasons for the choice of site – so every day special trains carried the armies of munitions workers, the majority of them women, to the works. Risley became one of Britain's largest wartime factories, shrouded in secrecy and absolutely vital to the massive war effort. With an internal network of light railways, and hundreds of buildings laid out along a grid pattern of roads, it was a dominant feature of the landscape, and hundreds of covered storage dumps and other facilities extended still further out into the moss.

On the earliest post-war maps the works was not shown, for reasons of

Risley Peat workers proudly pose with the characteristic tools of their trade.

Once the mosslands around Risley had been drained for farming and enriched they were incredibly fertile. Local farmers produced abundant crops of cabbages, leeks and celery which were supplied to nearby market towns, including Warrington.

continuing secrecy, but by the late 1950s the whole area was undergoing a progressive rundown as the needs of the military shifted into a cold war footing, and other munitions factories provided the bulk of national output. The decision was taken to close the Risley site and thus to create twin problems for the Warrington area. The first was how to find employment for what was still a large labour force. The second was what to do with more than two square miles of soon-to-be-derelict industrial land. Some parts of the site had found a new use. The United Kingdom Atomic Energy Authority made their new headquarters on the old site in February 1946 whilst a remand centre was opened at HMS Ariel, another former wartime site nearby.

As planning authorities and government departments debated the wider issues, one solution was increasingly favoured because not only would it potentially tackle these immediate issues but it would also meet what were seen as the wider needs of the north-west as a whole. Warrington, already a town of 65,000 people (with about the same number in the adjacent parishes), would be designated as a new town, with plans to expand its population to about a quarter of a million by the end of the century. This would provide an excellent way of taking overspill population from the Manchester and Merseyside conurbations (for this was the great era of slum clearance and urban renewal), it would generate major new employment growth for the district, and it would allow the complete redevelopment of the Risley site and nearby derelict land.

The new town was designated in 1968. Risley and its problems were top of

This photograph was taken by Warrington New Town Development Corporation to record the huge scale of the derelict wartime munitions site at Risley which would soon redevelop as Birchwood.

the agenda, although by this time the M6 had been opened and building the M62 was under way, and it was realized that the new motorway network, as well as revolutionizing accessibility and transport, would make the task of revitalizing the local economy much easier. Warrington new town was one of a generation of such projects in which new planning principles were applied. The existing large town would be a core but around it very large residential neighbourhoods were to be developed, each with a district centre at its heart so that local people had ready access to a wide range of services, including shopping, high schools, and cultural and entertainment facilities. Even in the late 1960s the full impact of the imminent explosion in car ownership was not appreciated, and it was assumed that these district centres would provide for most needs. The new town plan therefore defined an area east of the M6, south of the M62 and north of the main railway as a great residential unit, originally called Risley but (partly because of the connotations of the notorious Risley remand home and prison) soon rechristened Birchwood.

It was built from 1972 onwards, linked with the motorway and central Warrington by a new landscaped boulevard, Birchwood Way, which was to form part of a network of urban motorways that never actually materialized (that is why the road junction at Birchwood Park Avenue is so odd – it was designed as a multi-level interchange on a much bigger motorway network).

The housing areas were arranged so that they were smaller 'sub-sections' (such as Locking Stumps and Gorse Covert), each built around a smaller local centre with a primary school, and each with a circular through road from which small cul-de-sacs led off to individual residential groups. In the middle there was to be a massive industrial and commercial area, conveniently linked with each housing district by a footpath network. In reality, the conventional industry that had been anticipated failed to appear, because of fundamental changes in the structure of the British economy, so instead most of the allocated land was given over to the office developments and science parks of the late twentieth century. A new railway station, on the site of the temporary wartime platforms that had served the munitions works, is now served by most of the inter-city as well as local trains on the Liverpool–Manchester line. Though few would deny that Birchwood has had problems, it is an important example of late 1960s planning put into effect and in that sense the area has played a major part in the development not only of present-day Warrington but also of its historical significance.

Given the pre-1930s character of the district, it is particularly appropriate that the remaining areas of Risley Moss are now protected and conserved.

One ambitious scheme for Birchwood had limited success. The Spectrum arena and leisure centre was designed as a flexible venue for a variety of entertainments but the scale of the operation proved unsustainable.

The first phase of the new Birchwood shopping centre is seen here under construction in the 1980s. Set in the middle of nowhere, it would need the planned housing developments to be built nearby to sustain it.

When the Royal Ordnance factories were built in 1939–40 a large rectangular area on the eastern side of the site, north of the railway, could not be used because it was so waterlogged. While expensive drainage works would have been possible, the wartime conditions and urgency of the project meant that this was not feasible, so this undrained portion of the moss remained. Today it is a nature reserve, treasured for its specialized ecology and its landscape. Once such areas were commonplace and there were hundreds of square miles of such mossland in south Lancashire. Now, almost all that has been drained, reclaimed, improved, cultivated or built over, and obliterated. It is ironic, and fortuitous, that at Risley Moss, where there has been such intensive development and redevelopment in the past seventy years, a precious fragment of this primeval Lancashire landscape should survive.

CHAPTER SEVENTEEN

BURTONWOOD
AND WESTBROOK

Burtonwood lies at the north-western edge of the borough. Although it only came within the boundaries of Warrington in 1974, when local government was reformed, it had close ties with the town which went back to before the Norman Conquest. For example, Burtonwood township was part of the ancient parish of Warrington, and until the nineteenth century its chapel was subordinate to St Elphin's church. The township extended a good deal nearer to the town than is apparent today, for Bewsey and much of Dallam were within Burtonwood. The name was originally Burton, which means 'the enclosure around the burh [defended place]', although there is no evidence to indicate where such a location might have been. In the early medieval period the 'wood' was added, implying that Burton may have been elsewhere in the area and is now lost. The landscape around Burtonwood was flat and rather featureless, and there were extensive mosses on the poorly drained plateaux. By the eighteenth century these had been drained, and the township was noted for growing potatoes, turnips and other root crops and for supplying hay to the local urban markets. The village itself was very small, no more than a single street, now Chapel Lane, and it was well away from main roads.

Apart from Bewsey, the most important house in the township was the medieval moated complex at Bradley or Bradlegh Hall, on the southern side of the Sankey Valley. It dated back to at least the mid-thirteenth century and is one of the oldest manorial sites in south-west Lancashire. It was well-documented from the early fourteenth century onwards, when it was one of the main properties of the Haydock family, but in about 1414 it passed by marriage to the Legh family, the dominant landowners in late medieval Warrington. The house was very grand: a 1466 survey records a fine new hall, with new parlour, kitchens and bedchambers, a brew house and bakehouse, a turreted stone tower and a private chapel. There was also a separate defended gatehouse, the ruins of which still survive just inside the bridge spanning the moat: the detail of the remaining structure suggests that it was of very high quality, with vaulting and decoration, as befitted the residence of landowners of considerable social standing.

In 1759 the Sankey Navigation was built close to the eastern boundary of the township, but although it stimulated the rapid development of St Helens

this had little immediate impact upon Burtonwood itself. Alongside the canal was the great Sankey Sugar Works, which typified the way in which navigable water brought industry, for the raw sugar refined here came halfway round the world, but the fuel which powered the works was coal from St Helens, just up the canal.

Far greater consequences stemmed from the choice of George Stephenson's ambitious route for the Liverpool and Manchester Railway, which cut across the northern edge of Burtonwood and crossed the Sankey Valley by the spectacular viaduct at Earlestown which was one of the engineering marvels of the age. Opened in 1830, the railway had a direct impact because it encouraged prospecting and, in the mid-1850s, the opening of the colliery at Collins Green, immediately alongside the railway at the northern end of Burtonwood. By the 1890s this pit was one of the largest in south-west Lancashire, with a fan of sidings linked to the railway and with extensive coal tips which were beginning to encroach upon the adjacent flat fields. Half a century later Collins Green colliery, with its tips and sidings, occupied an area three-quarters of a mile by half a mile, with the main line running straight through the middle, and Burtonwood had become a sizeable coal-mining community, the only one in the area of the present borough. The coalfield does not extend southwards beyond the village, otherwise mining activity would certainly have approached nearer to the town.

Burtonwood's population increased rapidly as a result of this mining activity, from 831 in 1851 to 2,187 in 1901, and terraces of miners' cottages were built around the old village and in the vicinity of the colliery. There had been some other industries, such as nail-making and pin-making, and a little weaving, but essentially the township had been primarily agricultural until the exploitation of the coal. In 1867, partly in response to this increased population and growth in demand from thirsty miners, James and Jane Forshaw began brewing beer at Burtonwood. They sold a mere 20 barrels a week at first, but soon introduced a strategy of buying up public houses so that there was a guaranteed market for their beer (since the big companies, such as Greenalls, could otherwise use cutthroat selling and management techniques to force smaller competitors out of business). By 1907 Burtonwood Ales had a wide local market, supplying pubs and clubs between Prescot, Haydock, St Helens, Warrington and Widnes, and in the late 1940s, with some 285 tied houses, it had become one of the most successful of smaller provincial brewers. Very importantly, though, it fended off the threat of acquisitions from the big players and not only maintained its independence but also, astonishingly, outlived Greenalls, Walkers and most other local

This view of the Sankey Viaduct and Newton Locks appeared in an 1831 account of The most interesting scenery on the line of the Liverpool and Manchester Railway.

rivals, so today it still flourishes and has become a celebrated institution in its own right.

Life for the people of Burtonwood was turned upside down in the late 1930s. Just as, on the other side of town, the War Office looked for a site for a munitions works and found one at Risley, the RAF was seeking somewhere to build a major new aircraft and engine repair depot, ready for the war that everybody knew would come. The site needed to be flat (because the plans included a sizeable airbase), close to abundant labour supplies, with excellent road and rail links, and (though this was not specifically stated) as far as was feasible away from Continental Europe and the potential range of German bombers. In 1938 the flat fields of Burtonwood, which fulfilled all these criteria, were selected and work began on a new base with two runways, a complex of storage, production and repair shops, and administrative buildings. The base was fully operational in the autumn of 1940 but by that time the United States was sending supplies to Britain and Burtonwood was adapted to become the main reception site. When the Americans themselves joined the war they needed a new base in England and Burtonwood was

Sixsmith's Farm (later known as Tinker Hall) was requisitioned for the Burtonwood wartime base. Its occupants were philosophical about the situation: 'Then we got this blessed letter . . . from the Ministry of Defence so we knew the land was wanted for an aerodrome but not ready for the war. It was obviously a military take-over. Things just happened so quickly you hadn't time to be upset.'

An aerial shot of Tinker Hall site at Burtonwood in 1944 showing characteristic Nissen huts in the foreground. The original RAF site can be seen immediately in front of the two aircraft hangers in the background. A variety of aircraft are parked on the hard standing top right, including several B-17 Fortresses waiting to be serviced and returned to the operational squadrons.

chosen for massive expansion. In June 1942 the first Americans arrived, and in October it was formally handed over to the USAAF.

The statistics thereafter are awesome. In the summer of 1944 this was the largest factory in Europe, assembling bombers from prepackaged kits flown over from America, and over 10,000 people lived on the base. Only five months later the figure had risen to 18,000, and in a single week 269 aircraft rolled off the production lines. Burtonwood had three miles of runway, over 1,800 buildings, and enough accommodation to house a sizeable town. Its impact was far-reaching indeed. Not only was it a vital element in the successful war effort, but it also ate up half the open land between the village and Warrington, and the social consequences of all those thousands of Americans, overpaid, oversexed and over here, was dramatic. Within two months there had been a marriage with a local girl, while racial tensions emerged from the presence of numerous black servicemen – though by far the most serious racial prejudice was among the Americans themselves, and Warringtonians were commendably tolerant in refusing to accept the colour bar which the US military demanded. After the war the base was handed back to the RAF but, only two years later, the Americans resumed control as the cold war became rather too hot for comfort. Burtonwood played a key role in the Berlin Airlift and in 1953–8 it doubled in size as it became the largest American base in the world outside the US itself. Between 1948 and 1958 an average of 2.5 million people landed and took off from Burtonwood every year, and there were 30,000 flights a year from the base.

Then, very quickly, the Americans lost interest. Their attention switched from Europe to the Far East, as in the mid-1960s the Vietnam War grew inexorably. Colliery subsidence made the runway increasingly dangerous for large planes, while proposals to turn it into the world's largest ammunition store, serving all American forces in Europe, were dropped after vociferous local opposition. In 1965–6 the American forces pulled out, and the base was redundant. Although there had been plans to convert it into a new international airport to serve the Liverpool and Manchester conurbations that idea was quickly dropped because of the problem of subsidence. The road planners then decided that the main runway, long and straight and perfectly aligned, was tailor-made for the route of the new motorway, and at the beginning of the 1970s the M62 was built across the middle of the site. With the earlier demise of the munitions works at Risley, the collapse of the gigantic base and associated military and commercial complexes at Burtonwood was a key factor in the designation of Warrington new town. The area south of the motorway was quickly brought within the new town design, given over to major new residential areas at Westbrook, the peripheral road system and, most famously and most importantly, the first great edge-of-town shopping area in northern England.

Warrington was one of the first towns in England where out-of-town retail

USAAF Burtonwood's role in the Second World War was to keep the Allied planes flying, especially in the bombing raids leading up to the D-Day landings. The aircraft engine test beds ran twenty-four hours a day and the noise could be heard all over the town.

By the 1950s the Burtonwood base had become known locally as 'Little America' and Warrington girls jitterbugged with GIs in the local dance halls and went on to become GI brides. In the 1950s Burtonwood became America's gateway to Europe in the cold war era, and Cadillacs could be seen cruising on the streets of the town.

parks were built. The new town plan of the late 1960s assumed that shopping would continue to be focused on the old town centre, but by the time development was under way in the mid-1970s there was very strong commercial pressure for retail parks on the edge, close to motorway links and accessible only by car. The great Gemini complex was to reinforce Warrington's status as one of the most important shopping centres in the north-west. Fifty years after Burtonwood experienced a friendly invasion of 'Yanks', Swedish furniture giant IKEA arrived to set up its first UK store. Where once technicians assembled and repaired aircraft round the clock ready for war, shoppers could scramble to take home flat-pack furniture for peacetime homes. Other stores such as Marks & Spencer soon followed to make Gemini a major success story and cause traffic chaos nearby until a new motorway network was eventually built, partly on the old Burtonwood runway.

The land north of the new motorway, which had formed the larger half of the great military base, was left largely untouched until the late 1990s. Increasingly the new town authorities and, later, Warrington Borough Council, saw this as the last great development opportunity in the district, and planned a landmark development. The massive billion pound Omega scheme is intended to further boost the town's economic base, diversify its employment and generate jobs and wealth. If the ambitious scheme succeeds, another community will be arise to add to Warrington's diversity and help shape the next two thousand years of its history.

INDEX